Sons Without Fathers

OTHER BOOKS BY

James L. Dickerson
and
Mardi Allen

Screening Adoptive and Foster Parents

The Basics of Adoption

How to Screen Adoptive and Foster Parents
A Workbook for Professionals and Students

SONS
WITHOUT FATHERS

What Every Parent Needs to Know

Mardi Allen, Ph.D.

James L. Dickerson

SARTORIS LITERARY GROUP

In Memory of Mardi Allen's Father,

Edward Earl Allen

a man whose journey through life had more

to do with others than himself

CONTENTS

Introduction

"The world is not always a kind place. That's something
all children learn for themselves, whether we want them to or not,
but it's something they really need our help to understand."
—Fred Rogers, TV's 'Mister Rogers'

Whether children lose their fathers to divorce or death, or whether their fathers go to prison or abandoned them at birth, or were simply never in the picture—such as in artificial insemination—children who grow up without fathers in the home go through childhood at a distinct disadvantage.

We wrote this book to give hope to the millions of mothers who are raising children without fathers in the home and to the fathers who are no longer in the home. It is our belief that mothers can overcome those disadvantages with effective parenting tailored to their children's needs. We are convinced that most mothers want to do what is right for their children. If that does not always occur, it is usually because they do not always have the right information to do the right thing.

Specifically, this book was written for mothers who are raising children without fathers in the home; but it also is suitable for mothers and fathers who are contemplating divorce, lesbian mothers who are raising a son, and adoptive parents who are raising a son.

In 1968 there were about 60 million children in the U.S. under eighteen who lived with both parents, but by 2020 that number had slipped to 51.3 million. In 1968, there were almost 7 million children who did not live with their father in the home, but by 2020 that number had increased to 15 million, almost half of whom can be presumed to males who no longer have a male role model in the home.

Children of either gender suffer when their father is not living in the home with them, but the effect is greater for males because it deprives them of a male role model that defines their very existence. No matter how much females may miss having a father involved in their life on a daily basis, the fact remains that they have a mother for a role model and acquire a firm foundation for defining themselves in a world in which self-identity is crucial for survival once they leave home.

Sons who grow up *without* fathers have different needs, different experiences, and different life expectations from sons who grow up *with* fathers. Those differences begin in childhood and continue throughout life. Sons with fathers, absent physical or emotional abuse in the family, usually grow up to consider the world to be a friendly place with potential for great good. Without special parenting by their mothers, sons without fathers invariably see the world as an unfriendly place with potential for great harm, which is why we refer to them as Unfriendly World Children.

Some will grow up to accomplish great things.

Others will grow up to become ticking time bombs.

As young children, many of them shy away from strangers. They prefer to play alone. They distrust authority figures. And typically they expect the worst in any given situation. When they get older, they are sometimes combative and inextricably drawn to anti-social behavior. Rage is a common characteristic.

Of course, we all know men who grew up without their fathers and had wonderful lives. Some of the most famous and successful people in the world were Unfriendly World Children: President Barack Obama, President Bill Clinton, Robert Frost, Louis Armstrong, Jean-Paul Sartre, and Tom Cruise, for example. Unfortunately, they are the exception. So are those who are infamous for the dastardly deeds that they have committed: Serial killer Ted Bundy was an Unfriendly World Child, along with former Iraqi dictator Saddam Hussein.

The majority of Unfriendly World sons grow up to inhabit that vast middle ground between dysfunctional and exceptional. It is that middle group we had in mind when we wrote this book. When we refer to sons without fathers as having common traits, please understand that we are talking about the majority, not the exceptions.

You are probably familiar with the widely accepted notion that "boys are better at throwing balls than girls." That does not mean that every boy is better at throwing balls than girls—merely that most boys are better at that particular task. That is how you should view the statistics and opinions offered in this book.

They apply to *most* sons without fathers, not all of them.

Mental health professionals have known about the disadvantages of sons growing up without a father for years, but because each of the problems associated with that situation usually is diagnosed and treated separately, sons do not receive the full benefit that they would receive if the symptoms were combined and treated as one syndrome.

The Unfriendly World Syndrome—a phrase we coined—is a perspective that we are presenting for the first time in this book. It is our belief that the fallout of father-absent families can be lessened and possibly eliminated in some instances if corrective action is taken by mothers during childhood.

Shockingly, one in four white families in America is a single-parent household, while two/thirds of black families are single-parent households. Some have used that statistic to say that this is a black problem. That is not the case. Although the percentage of single-parent households is much higher for black households, the total number of children involved makes it largely a white problem nationwide.

In this book, we are putting the focus of our attention on parenting because the best way that a mother can help her son is by intervening at an early age. Once significant problems arise it may be too late for effective parenting to be the most significant factor in his life. At that point, professional intervention is crucial.

Over the past decade, there have been a number of books published on the subject of mothers raising children without their fathers. Most have done a good job of presenting basic information, but none, in our opinion, offer helpful advice on what to do to improve the odds for sons without fathers. Some books even offer harmful advice.

The question is not whether single mothers can raise sons, for we know for a certainty that they can; but whether, alone and without the father, mothers can raise healthy sons to have happy and productive lives.

We are convinced that they can—with help.

Instead of attributing their son's problems to bad luck, an act of God or bad fathering, mothers can empower themselves to make a difference. We urge mothers to use the information in this book to improve their sons' lives. We would like to see all sons without fathers be labeled as exceptional.

MARDI ALLEN

What I know about sons and fathers comes from my family and professional experience. My father had two daughters before his precious son, Bobby, was born. The night that Bobby was born, my dad walked through a horrible rainstorm to distribute cigars to his friends announcing the birth of his son. That night he also quit smoking so that he would be a better influence on his son.

My dad knew how important his behavior was as a role model for his son. While he was trying to teach my brother responsibility, my sister, Terri, and I (and sometimes my mother) were spoiling my little brother. We would do his chores, save our allowance to buy him toys, and take the blame for his mistakes. My dad loved his son enough to lovingly and firmly discipline him in spite of our protests.

Early in my college career I knew I wanted to seek a profession that worked with families. I volunteered at the hospital and at a facility for the mentally challenged. I began teaching fifth grade and found myself interested in the children's life beyond the educational process. I was broken hearted when only one parent attended the parent-teacher day. I wondered why my students' parents weren't interested in their children's education and why they did not want to meet the teacher. After that incident I realized that I wanted to expand my knowledge of family dynamics to include understanding emotions and behavior better. I pursued a doctorate in psychology, while continuing to work with children and their families in the church and community.

I've learned a lot from my professors and colleagues, but more from my patients. They bring their life stories to me, trust me to walk with them through their pain, and help guide them in seeking a better life. I've been particularly struck by the fatherless sons I've seen—fatherless either because the father doesn't want a relationship or because the mother has prevented the relationship. In either case, the sons have suffered the most. I've struggled to find resource books to recommend to these families to read, particularly for the father who wants to be a good father even if he doesn't live under the same roof as his children.

JAMES L. DICKERSON

Most of what I know about boys comes from having been one.

I have a degree in psychology, but I don't recall the subject of boys ever being addressed in the classroom. Chimpanzees and rats, maybe—but not boys. What I didn't learn about sons without fathers by being one—my father drowned in a boating accident when I was seven—I learned from working as a social worker in a child protection agency and by raising a son of my own. When my son's mother and I divorced, he became a son without a father. The fallout of divorce.

What I remember most about my father is the way that he included me in his activities, whether it was at work or tinkering with his car or going hunting and fishing or hanging out with his friends (who enjoyed a good game of poker in the back room of our garage). He never once said, "Now pay attention: this is what a man does." Instead, he showed me what to do by allowing me to watch him do what came naturally.

After my father died, it was my maternal grandfather, Audie, who made a conscious effort to teach me patience, respect for women and a strong work ethic, and my seven maternal and paternal uncles—Rex, R. P., George, Bill, Calvin, Luther and McCoy—who took up the slack and included me in their activities.

The interesting thing about my upbringing is how my mother

instinctively understood the principles that we are presenting in this book. She worked hard to find me male role models, whether it was with family or within organizations such as the Boy Scouts, where I not only learned how to tie knots and cook on a campfire, but how to throw a devastating right jab and an indefensible uppercut in Troop 53 boxing matches.

My mother did everything by the book (by a book that had not yet been written) and I can never thank her enough.

It is my hope that my experiences as a son without a father and my subsequent research on the subject will help mothers better understand their fatherless sons and help them to make decisions that will allow their sons to find happy and productive lives.

We think this is an encouraging book that offers hope to angry and frustrated mothers who are willing to put aside those feelings long enough to help their sons.

Sons Without Fathers

"One night a father overheard his son pray,
"Dear God, make me the kind of man my daddy is."
Later that night, the father prayed aloud, "Dear God,
make me the kind of man my son wants me to be."
Early the next morning, the mother prayed quietly to herself,
"Dear God, help me to show them the way."

--Unknown

CHAPTER 1

What Fathers Teach Their Sons

Growing up in New Concord, Ohio, future astronaut and United States Senator John Glenn enjoyed a close bond with his father.

"He joked a lot and made me laugh," Glenn wrote in his autobiography. "Part of the fun of being with him was that he was curious. He always wanted to learn about new things, and he would go out of his way to investigate them . . . He wanted to give me the curiosity and sense of unbounded possibility that could come from learning."

Glenn's dad, Herschel, owned a plumbing business and sometimes took him out on jobs with him if it did not interfere with his schoolwork. Glenn cherished those moments because they taught him about life and about becoming a man.

The summer Glenn turned eight, his dad invited him to go with him out of town to check on a plumbing job. On the way back home, they passed a rural airport and spotted an open-cockpit biplane parked on the runway. Intrigued, they stopped and got out to examine the airplane. Soon a man wearing a helmet and goggles walked over and asked them if they wanted to go for a ride.

Herschel turned to his son and asked a question that changed his life: "Want to go up?" Did he ever! Ever since Charles Lindbergh had made is famous transatlantic flight two years earlier, Glenn had fantasized about becoming a pilot. He asked his dad if he really meant it. "I sure do," answered his dad. "In fact, if you don't want to do it, I'm going anyway. So you better come unless you want to sit down here and watch."

Glenn and his dad climbed into the rear cockpit, where they shared a seat. The pilot got into the front cockpit and took off without any fanfare. One moment they were on the grass; the next moment they were in the air. They buzzed around Cambridge several times; then they returned to the airfield.

On the way home, Glenn couldn't get the experience out of his mind. His dad confided in him that it was his first flight as well. It was something he had wanted to do ever since he had served in France during World War I and witnessed airplanes in dogfights high above the battlefield. The fact that his dad would share that dream with him—and no one else—was a defining moment in their relationship.

Twelve years later, when Glenn was twenty and enrolled at Muskingum College, he came across a notice posted on a school bulletin board. It announced the formation of the Civilian Pilot Training Program, which offered to train students that wanted to become pilots. Both his mother and father were opposed to him enrolling in the program. They told him that it was too dangerous. They were not persuaded until the family doctor offered his opinion that it would provide their son with economic opportunities that he would not otherwise receive.

Put that way, his ever-practical parents relented.

Shortly after Glenn completed his training, he asked his dad to go up with him. He wanted to convince him that flying was safe. As he walked around the plane, checking it out, Glenn noticed that it sagged when his 230-pound father climbed into the cockpit. They no sooner started down the field for the take-off than Glenn knew that something was wrong. The throttle was wide open, but they were not traveling fast enough to clear the row of trees at the end of the runway.

"I was afraid to look at Dad, and didn't have time to do it, anyway," he later wrote. "I saw those trees coming toward me, and I began to have some doubt about whether we were going to get off the ground . . . I pulled back on the stick and the plane struggled up over the trees and dipped down again . . . With the engine running wide open we gradually got enough speed to finally start climbing. When I had the

nerve to look at Dad, he was unclenching his grip on the edge of the seat. But his eyes were twinkling behind his horn-rimmed glasses and he said, 'Like those exciting takeoffs, do you?'"

Glenn had the type of relationship with his father that every son has the right to expect growing up. His dad taught him empathy for others, math and physics through his plumbing business, how to relate to other men, and, perhaps most important, how to pursue his dreams. He taught him things about himself as a man that he otherwise might never have learned, especially concepts such as honor and pride.

Dad's Bag of Surprises

Before a mother can know how to compensate for an absent father, she must first understand the role he played in her son's life. It has been our experience that most mothers find the truth surprising, which is why so many of them make the same mistakes.

Fathers teach sons things that often are not taught by mothers: self-control and empathy, math skills, and respect for females. If that latter trait—"respect for females"—comes as a surprise to you, you are not alone because the myth is that women teach sons to respect other women. In truth, boys learn to respect women from their fathers.

It makes sense if you think about it. Studies show that males who grow up in families with an involved father do not have the same need to dominate women and create exclusionary, all-male activities as do males that grow up in families with an absent or uninvolved father. Statistically, they also lead happier lives. When happy and successful adult men are asked by researchers why they are happy and successful, they usually attribute it to the fact that they had happy and successful fathers. They seldom are able to explain the connection. It is just something that they seem to feel.

It has long been understood that fathers teach their sons math and sports skills, but only recently have researchers learned that fathers are instrumental in teaching their sons self-control and empathy, two critical skills associated with success and happiness.

19

In a twenty-six-year study that focused on the relationship between parental behavior in early childhood and "empathic concern" in adults, reported in the *Journal of Personality and Social Psychology*, researchers found that the most important correlation between parenting and empathy was the father's involvement in child care.

That finding astonished mental health professionals. In the absence of any existing research, they had assumed that empathy was a product of good mothering. To some people, empathy may sound like something that has no bearing on the real world, but empathy is what enables people to be law-abiding and compassionate citizens.

In addition to empathy, fathers teach their sons self-control, a quality that is closely linked to empathy. Mothers think of self-control as something that they impose on their son through discipline. Fathers think of self-control as something that they teach their son through good parenting; discipline is what they impose when their son does not learn self-control. Fathers are also relationship gatekeepers: They teach their sons how to relate to both males and females.

Mostly they do it by example, a good thing since little boys learn how to behave by watching other males, not by thinking about what is logical, proper or acceptable. Mothers have a difficult time teaching little boys how to behave around other males because they cannot do it by example, not without going to absurd lengths; they can only try to explain the concept to their sons with words, a communication that is doomed from the start. It works fine with daughters, who are more accustomed to talking things over with their mom, but it doesn't work with sons—and mothers sometimes have a hard time understanding why.

How many mothers have you heard say that their daughters are better listeners than their sons? The implication is that there is something wrong with the son.

You would think that sons raised by women would be more understanding of women's needs once they became adults, but it seldom works out that way. Statistically, a man who was raised by his mother is more likely to be abusive toward his spouse than a man who is raised by both parents. There are exceptions, of course, but that is generally the case—and our clinical experience supports that conclusion.

There are several reasons why mother-raised sons tend to be more abusive to spouses. They often blame their mothers for the fact that they grew up without a father, even when blame is not justified, such as in the case of death.

Later in life, that resentment often carries over to the spouse. Or they may never have learned how to argue with women. If a son never saw his father exert self-control when arguing with his mother, how could he possibly be expected to show self-control when arguing with his spouse?

Sons learn by "example" and girls learn by "explanation."

Those differences between the sexes continue into adulthood. The link between father-son involvement and math skills has long been recognized, but not until recently have studies proved that fathers also influence their son's verbal intelligence. No one understands why that is the case. It could be due to the father's problem-solving abilities or to certain behavioral qualities. Or it could be due to the fact that the child has more opportunities to study with a second adult in the household to share the parenting duties and to provide a more stable financial base. A live-in grandmother or aunt would also boost a boy's verbal abilities.

Men Have Poor Self-Images as Parents

Sometimes it is difficult for fathers to appreciate the impact they have on their children because the cause-effect of their actions is not as obvious as it is with mothers. It is helpful to remember that all fathers had mothers, and the natural tendency is for them to exalt the influence their mothers had on them, thereby exalting, by association, the influence their children's mother has on their son.

Most men have poor self-images as fathers. Yes, it's true: They might "know it all" when it comes to home repairs or the car, but they feel downright stupid when it comes to their children. Dads just don't get it. They consider their major responsibilities to center around providing for the family and protecting it from harmful outside influences. Women that proclaim anything associated with child-rearing to be their exclusive domain have helped perpetuate that myth.

It is true that a child's mother provides the first influence in her son's life, but that is largely because the mother has been given the biological mandate to carry the child. If newborns recognize and prefer the sound of their own mother's voice, over all others, it is because they have been hearing it for months from the womb.

During pregnancy, "the mother's voice gets through her body much more effectively than anybody else's voice," explains Dr. Lise Eliot. "So the baby is essentially doused with it for many months. Hearing really begins by the end of the second trimester. So, in a full-term baby you have three solid months of exposure to mom's voice. It creates a pretty strong preference in newborns."

Not until a few weeks after birth does a child recognize his father's voice. "Of course, it's all just a function of the amount of exposure," says Eliot. "If the dads would talk to the mom's abdomen every night, perhaps the child would recognize it. Somebody actually wrote me and said that it worked . . . I'm sure it is possible."

As further proof of the ability of fetuses to hear, Eliot points to studies that show that fetuses are able to identify different languages before birth. "Newborn infants prefer to hear their mother's native language over a foreign language," says Eliot. "In that case, they are tested not listening to their mom's voice, but to some strange woman's voice speaking both their native tongue and another language. Let's say it is an American child and they listen to a woman speaking English versus French—well, they actually prefer to listen to the English because it's already somewhat familiar to them. There is definitely auditory learning going on before birth."

Fathers downplay their parental role before their child's birth because they don't believe that it is possible to have a prenatal role. They are wrong, of course. Sons are tuned into family life before they are born—and they learn from those experiences.

We have seen parents carry on serious, life-altering conversations in the presence of their children in the mistaken belief that they are focused on their toys. Parents should not assume that a child is not listening just because he is playing and not making eye contact with them. On the contrary, parents should always assume that their children hear and understand everything they say in their presence. Whether dad realizes it or not, his son is learning serious lessons from him, even when that seems impossible.

Within hours of birth, infants can respond to, and in some cases, imitate both parents' facial expressions. Sons pay particular attention to dad, absorbing his every facial response.

Sons learn how to deal with other people by watching their father. How does he treat the son's mother? How does he treat his own mother? How does he react to other males? How does he treat people that he works with? Does he treat family members differently from strangers? Those are the life lessons that fathers teach their sons from infancy on, whether they realize it or not.

Faced with the loss of his father at an early age, Nobel Prize-winning French philosopher Jean-Paul Sartre pondered his uncertain fate:

> **Whom would I obey? I am shown a young giantess, I am told she's my mother. I myself would take her rather for an elder sister. That virgin who is under surveillance, who is obedient to everyone, I can see very well that she's there to serve me. I love her, but how can I respect her if no one else does? There are three bedrooms in our home: my grandfather's, my grandmother's, and the 'children's' . . . A young girl's bed has been put into my room. The girl sleeps alone and awakens chastely. I am still sleeping when she hurries to the bathroom to take her 'tub.' She comes**

**back all dressed. How could I have been
born of her?**

Sartre's insights, expressed in his autobiography *The Words,* are
those of a grown man, a literary giant who has come to terms with his
childhood; but they are pertinent for all sons. When Sartre's father died it
was necessary for his mother to move into the house with her parents,
where she was still treated as a child. Sartre saw what was happening,
absorbing every nuance, as children are apt to do, but its significance was
beyond his understanding at the time. How could Sartre respect his
mother when no one else did? How could he love her if she didn't love
herself? How could he trust her if she seemed unsure of her own
abilities? At the time, no one would ever have dreamed that a child that
age would have such thoughts. True, Sartre's intellect, even as a young
child, was superior to that of his peers, but the thought process he went
through to reach his conclusions is comparable for all children.

When the father is in the home, the son witnesses him treating his
mother with respect or disrespect—and he adopts similar attitudes
toward his mother and women in general. If the father is not in the home,
he observes how his mother is treated by her family and by strangers. If
they don't respect her, then it is unlikely that he will, either.

Why would he? Simply because she tells him to (remember, boys
learn by example, not explanation)? It would be nice if mothers were
provided with guaranteed respect by their children, but boys aren't wired
that way. The greatest assemblage of women in the world cannot
effectively instruct one six-year-old boy to respect his mother. That can
only come from his father—or from a suitable father substitute.

Dad's Dual Role: Bad Boy, Good Boy

When it comes to direct contact with children, the two areas that
society historically has set aside for fathers are discipline and play time.
Mothers feed and nurture the children, activities that involve a minimum

24

of interaction by children with their surroundings, while fathers serve as gatekeepers to all things beyond the mother's loving arms.

We will talk more about discipline later, but for the moment it would be helpful to understand that discipline and play are closely related in the eyes of children because they both involve a change in the life rhythms they experience with their mother. Almost always, dad is the "go-to" member of the family.

Playtime: Dad's the 'Main Man'

For infants, dad is the person who makes lots of noise coming into the room; the person who is always smiling and making eye contact because he has been away from his son all day. Sometimes he leans over and sticks his giant finger into the infant's tiny fist and stimulates his grasping reflex. Other times he lifts the infant into the air and swings him to and fro, taking son's breath away. Dad is always fun.

By contrast, mom always seems to come quietly into the room, so as not to awaken her son. She speaks in a soothing manner and tells baby how handsome he is. She makes eye contact when her purpose is non-nurturing in nature, but most of her time is spent feeding, bathing and changing baby, tasks that usually require her to gaze someplace other than the infant's eyes. Inadvertently, she frowns or gently chastises baby when he makes her nipple uncomfortable during breast feeding, when he kicks soapy water into her eyes during his bath, or when he makes an unusually pungent mess in his diapers. Mom is only human; she reacts to her environment, just as baby does, and complains about the "bad" things that he does. For that reason mom is not always fun.

For older children, those of pre-school age and older, dad is the parent who tosses balls with them, roughhouses with them, gets down on his hands and knees and pretends to be a horse, and the one who gleefully announces, "Everyone get ready—we're going to the circus!" For boys, the play activities they experience with dad are crucial for their long-term emotional and social development.

For adolescents, playtime with dad takes on more of a competitive edge. The skills he learned from dad as a youngster are used during adolescence as weapons with which to be competitive with dad and his peers.

Moms see competition as an event in which someone is hurt by being the loser; dads see competition as a means of solving problems while negotiating for dominance. Because moms don't want to see their sons get their feelings hurt, they try to protect them; dads understand that their sons' feelings will be hurt from time to time through competition, but they feel that the experience will prepare them for a world in which winning is more important than avoiding hurt feelings.

If your response to the above is, "well, the world just shouldn't be that way," then you are most likely a female. In father-intact families, dad usually wins the argument over whether a son should be exposed to hurt or failure. He is not insensitive to his son's feelings; he just wants him to learn to live with pain instead of avoiding it.

Interestingly, dad's attitude toward his daughter will be exactly the opposite; he will fight to protect her from hurt or disappointment, while the mom takes a similar position to the one that he took with their son. Typically, mom and dad will see no inconsistency in their opposing positions.

Of course, not all fathers are good playtime teachers. If they grew up as sons without fathers—and had difficulty learning how to play because they didn't have a father in the home—they will find it difficult to give their sons proper instruction. Even if they did grow up with a father in the home, they may have been taught by fathers that were overly critical of their efforts or prone to verbal abuse.

Psychologists Dan Kindlon and Michael Thompson touched on that in *Raising Cain*: "The problem-solving strategies that boys bring to adolescent and adult social situations are directly traceable to the lessons learned from dads on playing fields and in family dens. For instance, research shows that young boys who are aggressive and are low in pro-social behaviors—meaning they don't share—have fathers who are more likely to engage in angry exchanges with them, such as yelling back at a son who yells at them."

When fathers teach sons to play, hopefully it is to play fair and to let their actions, not their tempers, speak for them. The nightly news offers frequent reminders of what happens when fathers teach their sons the wrong lessons. We have all seen video footage of fathers charging out onto the playing field, screaming obscenities—or, even worse, fist fighting other adult males over calls made by officials.

For better or worse, dads program their sons to be good players or bad players.

When is Enough, Enough?

Psychologists Henry Biller and Mark Reuter once did a study on 172 college men to determine how often their fathers were at home when they were children, and how nurturing their fathers had been when they spent time with their sons. They found that well-adjusted students were likely to see themselves as dependable, trusting, practical and friendly, while poorly adjusted students were more likely to label themselves as aloof, anxious, inhibited and unfriendly. The most poorly adjusted students in their study had fathers who were home very little and were very nurturing, or were home a lot and were aloof and non-nurturing. The well-adjusted students had fathers who were at least moderate in both nurturance and availability.

"If you are not home much and are really affectionate and play with your child when you are home, he may feel very frustrated that you are frequently absent, and it may affect his personal adjustment; he may wonder why, if you appear to love him so much, you do not spend more time with him," Biller wrote in *Father Power*. "Conversely, if you are home a lot but are cold and distant, your child may feel that he is inadequate in your eyes, and he will feel very insecure. It would probably be better for a child with a cold, distant father to have him be home very little. At least the child would not be exposed to such consistently negative experience with a male."

It is unclear how much play Biller and Reuter included in their definition of nurturing, or whether the play included both physical and mental exercises, but their findings do indicate the fragile nature of a father's influence on his son. It is not enough for the father to simply be present in the home; to have a positive effect on his son he must engage him in physical or mental play. Biller and Reuter concluded that moderation in availability and nurturance offered the most beneficial balance.

A 1971 study, conducted by psychologists Peggy Ban and Michael Lewis at the Educational Testing Service in Princeton, New Jersey, found that fathers spent only about fifteen to twenty minutes a day playing with their one-year-old children. There are probably a lot of reasons for that: Fathers often feel embarrassed talking to or playing with infants; they don't feel competent handling small children; and they don't see such behavior as being compatible with their self-image as a male.

The older children get, the more time dad is likely to spend playing with them, especially if they are boys. Whatever their nurturing instincts as fathers, they are not as likely to spend a great deal of time playing with their daughters. Growing public awareness of the subtleties of child sexual abuse has something to do with that.

Men worry that their attentiveness to their daughters could be misconstrued and they worry that spending too much time with their daughters could affect their own masculinity, at least in the eyes of their male friends. Fathers don't have those same fears when they play with their sons. When it comes to play, men are still little boys at heart: they think that boys should play with boys, and girls should play with girls.

How Much Play Does It Take?

Obviously, the twenty-minutes-per-day average cited by the above-mentioned study is not enough. The amount of time that is adequate depends on the age of the child and the quality of the play that the father offers to the child. Preschoolers require more time than school-age children, as do adolescents, though getting *them* to make a time commitment is sometimes difficult. You can judge the time requirements for your child by terminating the play when he loses interest.

Quality also influences how much time a father should spend with his son. You are not playing with your son if you watch a football game while he rolls his favorite truck around your foot. Be actively involved. If your son is an infant, talk to him, make funny faces, sing to him, lift him up and down, get down on the floor with him and make strong eye contact. If he is school-age, go outside and play pitch with him, or horseshoes, or any number of physical games. Inside, you can play board games with him, cards, or even his favorite video game.

If he is an adolescent, you have to compete with his friends for play time and that will sometimes be frustrating. You cannot revert to your own childhood and say, "well, if he doesn't want to play with me, I don't want to play with him."

Think up more adult-oriented games for your adolescent son. Take him on fishing or canoeing trips. Go to the movies with him, if he will allow it.

Keep in mind that by the time your son is ten or twelve he will have selected a male figure that he admires and wants to pattern his life after. If you have not made yourself available for that modeling, he will look elsewhere. It could be a coach or a teacher, or, more likely, a much older boy.

The problem with that is that coaches and teachers have dozens, sometimes hundreds, of boys to supervise. They seldom have time to give more than passing attention to any single boy. They probably will not even know that your son has chosen them. As a result, they may disappoint him, creating more problems for you as a parent. Coaches and teachers can be effective role models within limits, but only if they do the choosing.

An attachment to an older boy could be your worst nightmare. Adolescent boys don't have finely-honed moral compasses. Since they are a work in progress, they are easily influenced by their peers. It is through these types of attachments that school-age boys are drawn into drug use, religious cults, and street gangs.

Boys who choose older boys as role models instead of their fathers, typically end up either as victims of peer abuse or as bullies to younger children.

Absent Fathers Stimulate Antisocial Behavior in Sons

We say this with benign sarcasm, but one of the best ways for parents to ensure that their son learn about the justice system is for them to divorce, then arrange for the son to be raised by the mother without the involvement of the father or a male role model.

Nationwide, 70 percent of the juveniles in state reform institutions grew up in father-absent homes, according to the U. S. Justice Department. That percentage is an average and varies from state to state, but it does paint a disturbing picture of the overall situation. Wisconsin has one of the highest percentages of children from father-absent homes in its juvenile detention centers, an astonishing 87 percent. Texas is close behind, with 85 percent of its youthful offenders coming from fatherless homes.

When individual crimes are broken down into percentages linked to father-absent homes, the figures become even more disturbing: 72 percent of adolescent murderers, 60 percent of rapists, and 70 percent of long-term prisoners grew up in father-absent homes.

What about the corresponding percentages—the 28 percent of murderers, the 40 percent of rapists, and the 30 percent of long-term prisoners—that reflect father-present homes? What does that tell us about the home lives of those adolescents? Some of them had wonderful parents and simply made bad choices. Others can be linked to fathers who abused them or their mothers. The impact of fathers on crime is undeniable, not just because of absence, but because of abuse as well.

In 1966, 165 students from the University of Maryland were studied to determine the effect of father absence on antisocial behavior. The students were asked if their father was ever out of the home, and they were asked to document the years that he was absent. Then the students were given an antisocial behavior test. When the tests and questionnaires were compared, they revealed that students with absent fathers had much higher incidence of antisocial behavior.

Any way you look at it, the father is key to the development of criminal tendencies in boys, whether by his actions as an abusive parent or spouse, or by his absence through divorce or death. That does not let mothers off the hook, however.

If mothers do not do everything possible to engage their son's father in his life—or, failing that, if they do not seek substitute male role models for their son—they bear some responsibility for the outcome. These days ignorance is no excuse.

Even when mothers are successful in encouraging their divorced husbands to spend time with their sons, they have a responsibility to their sons to know whether that time is being put to good use. An abusive father is worse than no father at all.

CHAPTER 2

Helping Your Son Understand Divorce

Tom Mapother never had a stable family life.

His father, Thomas, was an engineer and considered it his responsibility to relocate whenever the company needed him to participate in a new project. His mother, Mary Lee, saw her role as wife and mother as a supportive one, and she followed her husband about the country without complaint. During the first eleven years of Tom's life, the family, which eventually included three daughters, moved a total of seven times.

In his early years, Tom was a dreamer who sought adventures that he could enjoy alone. Mary Lee was a little bit like that herself. Each time they moved to a new city, she sought out the local playhouse and volunteered her time. At one point, she even established her own drama group. Once she realized that Tom enjoyed a rich fantasy world, she encouraged him to join her world by asking him to mimic his favorite television characters.

By the time Tom started school, it was apparent that he was not going to be a good student. What the family did not know then—but later discovered—was that Tom had a learning disorder. Simple reading was a nightmare for him. He didn't understand why he was different from the other students, only that he was not like them—and it hurt him to feel inferior to his classmates.

When Tom was twelve, Thomas and Mary Lee explained to their children that their marriage simply was not working out. As the children gazed at them in stunned silence, they announced plans to get a divorce. The children were devastated. Afterward, Thomas took Tom outside to play baseball, as if nothing had happened; he did it to distract Tom, but it only served to alienate him from a world that he no longer saw as safe.

Despite her best efforts, Tom's mother sometimes crumbled in the face of her son's expectations. When he notified her of his desire to play ice hockey, she said no, afraid that he would get his teeth knocked out. Undeterred, Tom secretly went to the ice rink at night and early in the morning before school so that he could prove to his mother that he could do it. They lived in Canada at the time, and hockey was considered a birthright. Tom's headstrong determination to play hockey, despite his mother's objections, is a classic example of an Unfriendly World son trying to create a friendlier environment. If Tom's father had been present, he probably would have encouraged his son's interest in sports.

Eventually, Mary Lee and the children moved to Louisville, Kentucky, where she and her husband had first begun their life's journey. It was not a glamorous homecoming, because she had little money and had to move her children into a low-rent house, the best she could afford on a sales clerk's salary.

Growing up, Tom had male friends, but he found it easier to trust females. That attitude can be attributed to the fact that after the divorce he grew up in a household in which he was the only male. When he needed comforting and understanding—and for a pre-teen boy that is fairly often—it always was offered by the females in his life. As a result, his adolescent concept of "maleness" derived from his mother's and sister's still-evolving concept of manhood.

By the time he was fourteen, Tom had some serious issues to resolve, both personal and educational. He was not doing well because of his reading problems and his mother did not earn enough money to enroll him in a private school where he could get specialized attention. In addition, he was having a difficult time envisioning where he would fit into the world as an adult.

The solution to all of his problems, he reasoned, was to become a Catholic priest. He enrolled in St. Francis's Seminary, a Franciscan order located near Cincinnati. There he could get an education and prepare for a vocation as a priest. Life changed radically for Tom at St.

Francis's. Instead of being surrounded entirely by females, he was in a female-free environment. He slept in a dormitory with about two dozen boys and he went to classes that were taught by male priests.

Tom only stayed at the school for one year. The brothers suspected they were losing him as a potential priest when they discovered that he was sneaking out of the dormitory to go to the homes of local girls. They knew that they had lost him for certain when he asked one of the brothers if he thought girls would be disinterested in him because of his diminutive stature.

When he was sixteen, Tom moved to New Jersey with his mother, his sisters—and his new stepfather, a plastics worker. Tom was slow to take to his stepfather and there always seemed to be tension between the two. Tom began looking for activities outside the family to occupy his time. At high school, he took up wrestling and soccer in an attempt to make new friends. He also tried out for the school production of Guys and Dolls. He landed the role of Nathan Detroit in the stage play and to the great pleasure of his mother and sisters he demonstrated a real talent for acting.

After the play, a talent agent approached Tom and told him that he had natural ability and should pursue a career as an actor. That was all the encouragement that he needed. After graduation from high school, he told his mother and stepfather that he wanted to go to New York to pursue a career as an actor. They encouraged him to go to college first, but Tom would have none of that. There was nothing in life that he wanted more than to become an actor.

The Tom in this story is Hollywood actor Tom Cruise. He is a good example of an Unfriendly World son who channeled his pain and alienation into creative and socially acceptable activities. Had his mother not encouraged his acting ambitions, both by example and by supporting his dreams, it is questionable whether he would have been able to self-treat his destructive impulses. Because his mother did the right thing in many instances, Tom was able to beat the statistics. Like any other Unfriendly World son, Tom had to learn to control his anger and his sense of social displacement.

Like most Unfriendly World sons, he has found it a continuing battle, as evidenced by his failed marriages and by his combativeness toward the news media. Almost every aspect of Tom's failed marriage to actress Nicole Kidman was pre-determined by his experiences as an Unfriendly World child. If the couple had received counseling based on that understanding, the outcome might have been different.

The vast majority of Unfriendly World sons do not turn out to be major stars like Tom Cruise, or like another successful Unfriendly World son, President Bill Clinton. What the success stories tell us is that there is hope for altering the outcome, if compensating actions are taken early in the child's life.

Tom was lucky in the sense that his mother made some good decisions along the way that opened the door for him to find success despite some formidable handicaps. She didn't have a guidebook to show her the way, but her instincts were right on target. Tom's son is lucky in that both his parents are doing everything possible to give him a friendlier world than Tom ever got to know.

Divorce Should be the Last Resort

Tom Cruise experienced great pain when life tore him away from his father, long before the natural course of separation should have occurred between a father and his son. If Tom had enjoyed the benefits of his father's influence in his academic achievement and his interests in sports, or if the family had lived closer to his father—it would have made a difference in his life.

Divorce should not be taken lightly. It should always be viewed as a problem, not a solution to your problems.

Not only will it bring major changes in the married couple's lives, it will change forever the lives of the children involved. Divorce is usually more problematic for boys than girls, since the children typically remain with their mother and whatever bond that already has formed with their father is usually damaged, if not broken. The devastating effects of separating children from their parents can never be undone. Of course there are abusive maritial situations that are more damaging than a divorce; but if a divorce is over something that could be forgiven and worked through, any effort put into repairing the marriage is time well spent if emotionally healthy children are desired.

When children are involved, mediation and counseling should be tried before any thought is given to divorce because the minute that the divorce-court gavel hits, life as children once knew it no longer exists. Although the father may not have been as active with his children as he should have been, his children were influenced by his presence in the home.

Divorce usually means physical separation from dad. When that happens, women suddenly assume a greater financial responsibility; they become the primary disciplinarian, tutor, household manager and sometimes have to move away from a familiar neighborhood. Often women are not as prepared for divorce as they thought they would be. Overwhelmed by the changes, perhaps still very angry and hurt, they sometimes relocate to another city, putting distance between them and their ex-spouse. Many children quickly find that they are separated by miles and eventually by emotional distance from their father after a divorce. Distance may help the spouses heal, but it makes it more difficult for the children to heal, especially if they enjoyed a close relationship with their father.

In his Unfriendly World a son of divorce feels rejected by the father. No matter how hard the father tries to reassure him, the son is likely to feel that way, even if the evidence of his father's rejection is circumstantial. The son has fantasies of how things could have been worked out, fixed or tolerated, to keep the family together. Sometimes during the separation period, the father realizes how important his relationship is with his children and he becomes more invested in them than ever before. Earlier, he may have felt inferior to the mother in terms of parenting skills, but now without her, he finds parenting to be easier.

Sometimes the father's confidence is boosted by being a successful parent in the absence of the mother. Ironically, in some cases divorce could have been avoided if the father had shown his enthusiasm for parenting prior to ending the marriage.

Once, in an interview with an eleven-year old Unfriendly Word son, we asked him if he believed that there were ever circumstances in which divorce is necessary, and he answered. "No—if your parents have problems they should go to a wedding counselor." Asked if he could have three wishes, he responded: "1) that Mom and Dad would get along better; 2) that dad would move closer to us; and 3) that I could get a new skateboard." In this case, the dad had not moved since the divorce and had kept the same job in the family business for fifteen years, but the mother had taken their children and moved to three different states. She often made statements about not wanting to live in the same town as the children's father because she hated him. Even though the son was aware of the facts, the physical distance made him feel rejected by his father. The mother no longer had to see her ex-husband, which made her happy; but her decision did irreparable harm to a son who desperately needed to see his father.

Billy's Journey into Adulthood

For most of his early life, Billy lived in a seemingly perfect world. He went to the best schools, where he reveled in the sight of his mother and father sitting together in the bleachers whenever he played soccer, and he enjoyed the friendship of neighborhood children who shared his interests.

All that came to an abrupt halt when he was eight years of age, when his parents sat him down before dinner one evening and told him that they were getting a divorce. It happened as quickly as changing television channels. One minute he had a happy family; the next minute he had a broken heart. It made his head hurt to even think about it.

After that day, *everything* in Billy's life changed. His father moved out of the house and into a downtown apartment, and then later moved to another city. He knew nothing about the "other woman" in his father's life because his saintly mother protected him from that in the belief that it would turn him against his father.

Billy and his mother lived in the same house for nearly a year. Then they moved to a smaller house in a different neighborhood, where he was enrolled in a new school. Making new friends was difficult for Billy. He avoided participating in any group activities, preferring instead to play with one friend at a time, typically the one who gave him the least amount of grief over not having a father in the home. That tendency to deal with people, one at a time, stuck with him for the rest of his life.

Billy's father spent time with him every weekend in the months following the divorce, but when his employer transferred him to another city, the visits scaled back to once a month. In time, they tapered off to weekly visits only during the summer months.

Fearful of Billy becoming too isolated, his mother encouraged him to join the Pee Wee football team (the school did not have a soccer team). Reluctantly, he did as she asked. After a few practices, his mother felt guilty about him not having a father on the field like most of the other boys, so she volunteered to assist the coach during the practices, a decision that subjected her son to even greater ridicule.

The other boys gang-tackled him and gang-blocked him, always uttering choice phrases about his mother and his "manhood" as they nailed him to the ground.

"What's the matter, Billy? Need your mother here so you won't get hurt?"

"Baby needs his mother! Baby needs his mother!"

Billy got into so many fights with the other players that he was kicked off the team. His mother encouraged him to try out for the Little League baseball team. He made the team, but it was the same thing all over again, primarily because so many of the football team members also went out for baseball. Instead of Billy getting gang-tackled and gang-blocked, he was deliberately hit with the baseball by the pitcher when he was at bat and by other team members when they threw the ball to him.

By the time he was twelve, Billy had given up any hope of participating in organized sports, but because he liked sports, he continued to play sandlot games with those classmates that didn't go out for organized sports. One boy had leg braces because of a birth anomaly. Another boy was obese and could not run without falling down. Yet another boy was deaf. A bright child, Billy got the picture and concluded that others saw him as handicapped because he did not have a father.

Billy's mother decided not to remarry in the belief that it would protect him from the trauma of having a stepfather, but she did nothing to find him male role models, preferring instead to do those things herself. As a result, Billy went through childhood and then into early adolescence without ever being in a position to observe adult males on a day-to-day basis, outside of his male teachers at school.

Billy had no real outlet for his pent-up frustrations. He had no adult males to talk to about the issues that troubled him the most during puberty—girls, bullies, sports, and career goals. His mother told him to be "sweet" to girls so that they would like him and she told him to turn the other cheek to the bullies that taunted him.

Billy's classmates laughed at him wherever he was "sweet" to the girls in his class. When they saw that he would not fight back if bullied, they made a joke out of pushing him down and tripping him on the playground.

By the time he turned sixteen, his most distinguishing characteristic was his quick temper. He always seemed to be angry about something. He had quit playing sandlot sports several years earlier, so he had no socially acceptable way of displacing his anger. As a result, instead of studying and applying himself in class, he spent a lot of his time daydreaming about what he was going to do to even the score with his "enemies"—and that list was composed of just about everyone he ever knew, except his best friends.

Billy got through high school, but just barely. He often got into trouble for talking back to teachers and for ignoring the dress code. When the principle instructed male students not to wear their hair past their collars or down to their ears, he shaved the back and sides of his head and defiantly brushed his remaining hair down over his eyes.

What Billy's behavior indicated was that he was still suffering from depression over the loss of his father and over his inability to fit in with other males who had fathers living in the home. He didn't express that depression as sadness; he expressed it by acting out in a variety of ways—and by doing poorly in school. Billy's story represents one of the "blind spots" in public perception about sons without fathers. Losing a father to divorce is just as powerful as losing a father to death, or never knowing a father.

If Billy's mother had better understood what he was going through, she could have taken actions to deal with his continuing sense of loss and better advised him on his relationships with his classmates. She did not realize that boys often express depression through angry outbursts, poor school achievement and overall frustration, rather than crying and saying, "I'm unhappy!" She was totally devoted to her son—indeed, he was the focal point of her life—but her good intentions were not enough to protect him from the natural effects of fatherlessness.

In this situation, her decision not to remarry would have been a good one if she had also pursued a strong male role model for her son outside the home. Likewise, her decision to encourage his interest in sports would have been a good one if she had then stepped out of the picture and allowed nature to take its course. She went to great lengths to protect her son from the truth about his father, but it never occurred to her that the truth could have been beneficial in helping him understand his father's absence.

Billy's mom possessed great love for her son, but that love went through a bad-information filter that devalued it. As a result, Billy drifted so far into unfriendly-world territory that he stumbled into adulthood at a disadvantage.

Coping with Family Breakup

Most couples enter into marriage assuming that they will remain together forever, enjoying a loving, productive life in which their hopes and dreams for each other are expressed through their children.

Unfortunately, several years later and after the birth of children, many couples find that their initial assumptions were inaccurate.

They no longer enjoy one another. They find fault easily and drift further and further apart. Neither can recall their feelings of initial attraction, nor when their feelings took a 180-degree turn. As the distance between the two increases, child-rearing stress adds more conflict to an already unhappy couple. What seemed to be minor differences in the early years of their marriage become overwhelming, unsolvable conflicts.

When the natural flow of life is interrupted by the breakup of a family, there are always consequences. Hurt is perhaps the most common consequence of these shattered dreams. Often this emotion is poorly managed and hard to overcome.

Families can be shattered by partners making poor decisions, losing sight of priorities, using anger to display frustration, avoiding dealing with enviable conflicts, or a variety of other reasons. Many couples rush into the process of dissolving their marriage quickly, without evaluating the pros and cons for all involved. Later, many divorced couples realize that if they had spent as much time and energy trying to improve their marriage as they spend starting over, their marriage would never have failed.

The Language of Divorce

Often when parents have discussions with their children to inform them that a divorce is eminent, they make statements like, "Mommy and Daddy have stopped loving one another, but neither of us will stop loving you." Or, "The divorce has nothing to do with you—it's just that we can't get along."

Children do not understand when parents try to explain their love for them by saying that they love them because they are "blood relatives," while the mother and father are not blood relatives—and therefore have no obligation to love each other. Children are simple in their thinking. They attribute love to those who are physically close to them—those who care for them and help with their homework. For sons,

41

love has more to do with actions than what type of blood flows in their veins. Don't forget, you have to show sons what you want them to learn—words just won't do.

Soon after the "divorce news" is announced, many angry couples do everything possible to hurt one another, including using their children to lash out at the other. The range of conflict varies from being totally absent, to fighting constantly in front of the children, and repeatedly going to court to resolve minor issues.

They refuse to cooperate when making decisions about the children. They criticize the other in front of the children. And they make loyalty demands of the children. We advise parents in conflict to: **Get Over It** . . . and if they can't do that, then we advise them to **Keep It To Yourself**. Either way, they should just . . . **Move On.** For the children's sake, they should either try to get along or just fake it. Their son's needs should come first.

Children need attention, physical presence, affection and guidance from both their parents. They need to feel protected by them, assured that the parents are capable of taking control when necessary. Sons need to be in the presence of a male parent who will be available to encourage him, take him places, talk to him, and guide him. The most qualified teacher for a son is his dad. Whether intentionally or not fathers teach their sons a value system, coping strategies, self-control and self-reliance. Even when there is limited contact, sons will find themselves becoming their dad over time.

Most adults understand the need for children to have contact with both parents, but many ignore that need. Parents should encourage the non-resident parent to participate as much as possible in their son's life. Any parent that intentionally hinders another's parent/child relationship is guilty of abuse, however subtle.

A solid parental relationship is built on emotional support, consistent expectations, and firm, but loving discipline. Parents should not compete for "parent of the year" awards from their children, but instead contribute their own uniqueness to the parenting mix. Children need both parents to contribute equally, but differently.

Hurt Disguised as Anger

Initially, a divorcing couple may see anger as their primary emotion, rather than hurt, but over time it becomes apparent that the hurt of losing the dream of marriage and family is the underlying emotion that drives most destructive behavior. Often the anger, frustration, and blaming are substitutes to simply screaming out, "It hurts to lose my dream!"

The expectations of modern mothers have shifted from homemaker, caregiver and supportive spouse to all of the above, plus co-breadwinner. Improved job opportunities, relaxed divorce laws, and changing public perceptions of female roles have been major contributors to the increase in divorce over the past thirty years.

As women have developed a strong sense of independence and achieved self-sufficiency, many conclude that the hurt of ending a bad marriage is better than staying in the marriage. Woman have realized that they can manage employment outside the home, be the primary caregiver for the family, and manage the household demands with often little or no assistance from a spouse. As a result, it is often the woman who initiates divorce proceedings.

An angry wife's divorce proceeding may be acting-out behavior on her part based of some initial hurt over her husband's affair, lack of attention, his anger or other unacceptable behavior. Often when women delve below the surface, they find that there were many contributing factors that lead to the demise of their marriage. Typically, the actual behavior that caused the divorce was only a symptom of other problems in the marriage. Of more importance, usually, is the "little stuff" in a marriage that snowballs into a major conflict.

'How Could I Have Been So Wrong?'

Randall and Teresa were married after six months of dating. He was handsome, seemed very carefree, and enjoyed life to its fullest. Teresa also liked to have a good time, had a ready smile, and was willing to make time for Randall in her busy schedule. She was strikingly beautiful and enjoyed the attention her looks brought her.

They had an uneventful courtship, marked by Randall's frequent phone calls and insistence on spending every possible moment together; he appeared to be slightly obsessive, but rather sweet early in the romance. When she was busy, he mumbled a little, but eventually seemed to get over it. Once or twice, a hint of jealousy crept in, but was quickly dismissed with a romantic evening or a special gift. The terrific time they shared seemed to overshadow the seemingly small details of adjusting to one another.

Randall and Teresa had a large wedding, with lots of friends and family who celebrated with dancing, food and alcohol for most of the day. Several times during the reception, Randall advised Teresa to be more careful because her wedding dress was too revealing. She barely acknowledged his comments and continued to enjoy the reception with her friends, many of whom did not even know Randall. He seemed a little aggravated when she danced with other men and he made a couple of remarks about her hugging and kissing too freely. Teresa blew him off as being nervous about the wedding. She truly loved Randall and she knew that Randall would never have to be concerned about her being interested in another man.

Later in the afternoon, Randall angrily huffed, "two can play at this game." He danced with every attractive female in attendance and made a point to hug and kiss each one. Teresa had little concept of Randall's jealousy until they left to catch the plane to go on the honeymoon. Randall barely spoke all the way to the airport and as soon as he got seated on the airplane he took a pillow and promptly went to sleep. Teresa felt disappointed because she was still hyped by the excitement of the day and wanted to chat with Randall. For a brief, panic-stricken moment, she pondered the question: "How could I have been so wrong about this man?"

The honeymoon seemed almost eerie to Teresa, as if she was with a man she barely knew. He had a negative comment about almost every outfit she wore. Admittedly, she enjoyed wearing short skirts, but she felt that her necklines were not too revealing. Teresa had always turned heads when she entered a room and she had no intention of trying to play down her beauty just because she was now married.

The night before they returned home, Randall finally expressed his feelings. He said he was hurt that Teresa was "still" dressing so sexy now that she was "no longer" available. He accused her of displaying a lack of respect for him by dancing, kissing and hugging strangers. Teresa protested that none of the men at the reception were strangers. She had known all of them many years and probably could have had her pick of any of them to marry. She expressed anger that he thought he could now dictate to her.

Once the newlyweds returned home, they settled into a routine. Within three years, they had two precious sons. After each baby, Teresa returned to work as soon as possible, although Randall protested. As her resentment for Randall grew, so did his demands. She vacillated between feelings of guilt and anger.

Teresa became more and more discontented with Randall. By their fourth wedding anniversary, she equated him with constant criticisms. She, too, started expressing jealously, but hers was over his freedom to play golf, his willingness to nap on the couch every evening while she did housecleaning, and his lack of responsibility for the children.

One evening, after a nice anniversary dinner—and an expensive gift from Randall—she announced that her anniversary gift to him was a divorce. Randall was totally caught off guard. Hurt and frustrated, he accused her of having an affair, of never loving him and being extremely selfish. Randall could not accept that he had contributed to the demise of their marriage. He expressed disappointment with her behavior, beginning with their wedding reception. He explained that "he never dreamed" that she would continue to flirt with men, want to travel so much and be away from her family, and wear sexy clothes to attract attention.

Clearly, Teresa and Randall had not done a very good job of analyzing their odds of success prior to marriage. Now after four years of misery and two sons, Teresa wanted out. Although it is not the focus of this book to advise young couples on mate selection, it is important to emphasize the earlier any couple faces the reality of their differences, the better for all. Why couldn't Randall and Teresa have recognized their differences before marriage, or at least before having children?

In the midst of romance, it sometimes is difficult to anticipate problems. Teresa's independence was clear from the onset, as was Randall's possessiveness, but the awareness of those potential problems was overshadowed by the thrill of the courtship. Prior to marriage they both looked the other way to incompatible behavior. As a result, it will be their sons who pay the price for those errors in judgment.

Teresa and Randall now face a much more complicated life as they deal with divorce, providing for their two sons, maintaining separate houses, and meeting increased financial demands. When Randall picks up the children, he seems compelled to sneer at Teresa's clothing, insinuating that she's trying to be sexy. She makes the interactions no easier with her comments about dating men that Randall had falsely accused her of seeing when they were married. They have allowed the pain of their marriage failure to hinder their responsibilities as parents.

By remaining stuck on the question, "How could I have been so wrong?"—and by continuing to fight the same tired, old battles—Teresa and Randall ignored the basic fact of divorce as children are concerned:

The divorced parent's ability to get along determines their children's adjustment!

Randall and Teresa's divorce was traumatic for everyone involved. In the end, Teresa was granted custody of the children, with Randall given liberal visitation privileges. That was not what Randall wanted, so he spent endless hours and money trying to find fault with Teresa in order to reverse the custody decision.

Angered by that, Teresa became obsessed with informing the children of Randall's shortcomings. She ridiculed him in the presence of

46

the children, avoided taking his phone calls, and never told them that their father had called.

This is a familiar example of how parents rob their sons of hope for future happiness, contribute to their long-term emotional problems, and increase the risk of health problems.

Timing is Everything

With the exception of ending an abusive marriage, most divorcing couples follow a series of predictable stages in recovery. The difference is in the timing. Most partners do not work through the hurt at the same time, nor are they very concerned about how well the other party is doing. Anyone who has gone through a divorce can empathize with the sensation of drowning in a gulf of confusion and doubt.

After the anger subsides, each spouse typically feels a sense of grief, even when divorce is what was desired by both partners. The end of a dream, the broken promises, and the loneliness that comes from separation, all contribute to the pain of divorce. Even when there is a strong support system available, both partners will face some grief over the loss of the marriage promise.

When a third party is involved, there is sometimes a misperception that the nightmare will soon be over and new life is on its way; but seldom does divorce that is due to infidelity result in a happy re-marriage. Often the lover only serves the purpose of giving the divorcing spouse the courage to do what has been desired for some time.

When therapists discuss the causes of divorce with couples, they usually discover that their reasons for wanting a divorce have little in common. Women and men often interpret the underlying conflicts that contribute to divorce very differently. When you are talking to them, it sometimes seems as if they are in different marriages.

No matter what the perceived causes of the divorce, each parent needs to make a concerted effort to rise above the hurt in order to find a reasonable level of respect for one another and learn to get along for the

Reported Causes of Divorce

Women's Report of Male Behavior	Men's Report of Female Behavior
Lack of communication	Too much criticism
Poor money management	Too wasteful
Sexual problems (lack of affection)	Sexual problems (infrequency)
Lack of shared interests	Too much closeness
Too much alcohol use	
Lack of anger control	
Infidelity	Infidelity

children's sake. A basic requirement of good parenting is doing whatever it takes to "get over" the desire for continuous conflict.

Unfortunately, each individual must sort out his or her feelings at their own pace. Ex-husbands often appear outwardly oblivious to the recovery process, whereas research suggests that men have a less effective adjustment than women. Men tend to externalize their feelings by driving too fast, drinking too much, seeking new sex partners, and expressing themselves through more irresponsible behavior. Women, on the other hand, are more likely to seek therapy to deal with the emotional impact of the trauma, while looking for new romance and new employment opportunities. Often the "out of sync" interactions common to divorce are characterized by conflict and revenge.

Being overly friendly, or staying in close contact, are not necessary for divorced couples, but maintaining respect for the once-loving relationship that created the children is crucial to their emotional health. Given that from 85 to 90 percent of the children of divorce end up living with the mother—and the fact that parents discipline the same sex child more effectively—greater concern should be shown for sons of divorce.

Divorcing couples with sons should be aware that:

* Boys witness conflicts between parents more often than girls, before and after the marriage breakup.
* Boys are less likely to be emotionally nurtured during divorce proceedings.
* Boys make less favorable adjustments than girls during the first year.
* Boys are more aggressive, do poorer in school, and display more social problems following divorce.

The age at which a boy experiences divorce has a bearing on his reaction. Boys aged six to eight are typically very upset by divorce, and feel a great deal of sadness and rejection. By that age, they have formed a strong bond with their father and often weep and experience feelings of profound loneliness without their dad.

Pre-teen boys who experience a family break-up usually report an overwhelming sense of loss, despite the fact that their outward behavior sometimes suggests extreme anger. Sons feel short-changed without an adult male who is readily accessible. They typically act out, while figuratively screaming for society to right what they see as a personal wrong. They often take sides in the divorce dispute, while showing belligerence and confusion, only to vacillate between the parents as the issues change on a given day.

Often sons believe they possess the power to reunite their parents. No matter what age the divorce occurs, many sons of divorce never let go of the hope that someday their parents will find their way back together. This unrealistic hope often hinders the acceptance of a step-parent. It can also get in the way of enjoying satisfying relationships with both parents. A son or daughter that focuses only on a goal of reuniting the family loses valuable time and emotional energy on fiction. Parents must help the child fully understand and separate the two relationships. It is only with time and experience that the sons of divorce begin to see life beyond divorce.

Parents Should Get Over It
. . . The Kids Have

It takes time for most of us to recover from a hurtful situation. It is when parents can't let go of the pain that damage is inevitable. We've seen many couples that pretend that their arguments with each other are "for the children." It is not until the layers of hurt and anger can be peeled away that such individuals can see that they have been using their innocent children as human shields.

Children are often more resilient than adults. Depending on the age of the child—and the amount of parental support they receive—they can achieve a successful transition to a new family configuration. In most cases, children can forgive and then move on quicker than their parents. Just as parents move through certain stages after a divorce to achieve a healthy level of acceptance, so do children. At each stage, the child must acknowledge an important fact of life, which, once addressed, can help him move on to acceptance. Those stages are:

- **It's over.** The marriage has ended. The child must stop denying that his parents are just going through a phase or that things will get back to normal soon. To keep slight hope alive gives children unrealistic hope; once the child understands "it's over," he can figuratively bury the fantasy.

- **You are powerless.** You didn't cause it and you can't fix it. Some children suffer extreme self-blame, feeling responsible for the family break-up. He may think, or actually say, "If only I had been a better student," or "If only I had behaved better," and so on. He may also feel that he has the power to re-unite his parents.

- **You do not have to choose.** You can love both parents. It is important that a child be allowed to remain close to both parents so that he doesn't feel that he has been divorced from either of them.

- **Believe that things will get better.** Sons are full of hope and will believe in a better tomorrow with a little encouragement. Both parents should reassure their children that "things will get better," even if they themselves have not reached that level of acceptance.

We know a twelve-year-old boy who devised an elaborate plan to "trick" his parents into getting back together after four long years of divorce-court battles. He believed he could conjure a scheme to re-unite two people who no longer loved one another, even though both loved him. That child clearly is stuck in his path to re-adjustment. Although the parents continue to have conflicts, he offers ideas on how they could get back together, clinging to the unrealistic hope that they will work things out and re-unite his fantasy family.

Not until a child has dealt with the facts can he finally accept the permanence of the divorce. This is not a loss of hope evoked by depression, but rather a calm realization that his parents are no longer capable of having a happy life together. The child must learn to respect his parent's decision to dissolve the marriage and then turn his hopes for happiness in a different direction.

Children of divorce often have difficulty developing hope for future relationships. Some may progress through all the stages of acceptance of the parent's divorce, up to the final step, but then fail to ever advance to a point where they can believe that things will get better. Most children would benefit from psychotherapy when families break-up. Professionals know how to assist a child through the crisis of a family break-up and can help him confront the peripheral issues that often escape the attention of parents.

It's No Longer About You

Once the dissolution of the marriage is eminent, parents should turn their full attention to the really important members of the family—their children. These are the innocent bystanders who are involuntarily dragged into the mix.

In their book, *Psychological Experts in Divorce, Personal Injury, and Other Civil Actions,* Marc Ackerman and Andrew Kane encourage attorneys to help their clients understand the reality of divorce. Often couples are caught off guard by the financial strain divorce causes. They fail to realize that living apart will decrease the time each gets to share with the children. They seem to forget that holidays are limited, and shuffling children back and forth is difficult and inconvenient. During divorce, many hurt and angry couples are more focused on getting out of the marriage, or getting back at the spouse, than evaluating the long-term effects of their actions on the children.

Couples should consider joint custody if they are capable of working together in the best interests of their children. A couple that is able to respect each another and consult on issues concerning their children will up the odds of having well-adjusted children. When children observe their parents sharing parenting activities, even after divorce, they can be free to openly love each parent without fear. However, in some cases, even when the couple can get along, joint custody is not feasible due to work obligations or distance.

As much as possible, every effort should be made to keep both parents involved in the decision making process. Children need to feel that both mother and father are partners in parenting, even though they may no longer be husband and wife. If at all possible, parents should make an effort to live in close proximity to one another. Living in the same town, even in the same neighborhood, ups the odds for good adjustment.

Invariably, there are times when there is a need for a sitter. Parents should not rule each other out as sitters, simply because they are divorced. Of course, it is both disrespectful and inconvenient for a divorced parent to call on the other parent at the last minute to baby-sit. Whenever possible, offer the ex-spouse time with the children instead of using a babysitter.

Parents need to be aware that frequent moves have an adverse effect on the child's psychological development. Moving from place to place forces children to enroll in numerous schools, make new friends, and adjust to a new environment—and those stresses are not advised while they are simultaneously trying to re-adjust to family changes. Maintaining sameness is helpful during times of upheaval for children. Children need to maintain a sense of security, predictability and comfort.

This is often provided by living in the same neighborhood, attending the same school, and participating in an established circle of friends. With so much of their life crumbling around them, a safe haven is more than a comfort—it is a necessity.

Researchers recommend that courts show favor to the "psychological parent." By that, they mean the parent that is able to take charge while showing understanding and an appreciation of the rules that are necessary for raising healthy children. Data suggests that children are happier, more self-reliant, and better able to meet life's challenges more effectively, when parenting has been consistently firm and loving.

Parents need to limit the child's power to control decisions.

When a parent is emotionally weak, there is a tendency for the parent to lose control and allow the child to seize power. Often emotionally distraught adults turn to their children for support, friendship and advice. Although most children will readily accept such offers, they innately do not want the responsibility. Children should never be put in a position where they have to "parent" the parent, or become their friend and confidant.

Children should be encouraged to love both parents freely.

Parents who are immature and selfish seek revenge by competing for the love and loyalty of their children. By playing such games, the parents create damaged children. After a divorce, a child is usually confused and unable to make rational decisions about his parents. Feeling powerless and confused, a child is easily influenced and swayed to one side, then the other. An angry, vindictive parent will reap joy from a child refusing to visit the other parent. However, this and should not be tolerated. Neither parent should allow criticism of the other parent. We totally agree that children should speak openly about both parents, but petty criticisms should not be allowed. Children must see their parents as a united front, even after divorce.

Parents must work together to teach values to their children. They should never ask their child to lie for them or keep adult secrets. They should not be fooled into thinking that they can display inappropriate temper outbursts and then turn around and teach their child to control his temper. Parents that don't like the person in the mirror won't be pleased with their children, either.

Mothers, take this unscientific test to determine if you are promoting a good relationship between your son and his father. If any of the following statements apply to you, then answer "yes" and tally your responses.

1. I can't let go of my anger toward my son's father.
2. When my son is with his father, I am constantly worried.
3. It is hard for me to believe that a man that has treated me so badly could be a good father to my son.
4. My son has too many of his father's negative personality traits.
5. My ex argues with me every time we speak.
6. He only takes his son on the weekend to upset me.
7. My ex's goal is to cause trouble between me and my son.
8. My son always misbehaves after time spent time with his father.
9. I resent having to deal with homework, discipline and other problems, while my ex takes my son out to "fun things."
10. My son would be better off if his father never came around.

If you answered "yes" to more than three of the above statements, then it is time for you to stop and think about what you are doing. "Yes" answers are a good indication that you are focusing more on your best interests than your son's best interests. Acknowledging that you have destructive feelings about your ex-husband can lead to a better understanding of yourself. It is important for you to look beyond your negative feelings toward your son's father in order to provide for your son's needs.

CHAPTER 3

When A Father Dies

Robert Frost and his poetry are associated with rural New England, but he began life as a city boy in San Francisco, where he often roamed the streets with his father, Will Frost, a confirmed walker who was known to pack a Colt revolver in his belt as he made his rounds. William was one of the more eccentric editors at the Daily Evening Bulletin. Just prior to Robert drawing his first breath, Will sternly warned the attending doctor that if anything went wrong he would shoot him—and he meant it, too.

Will often took his son with him to work at the newspaper.

One of the poet's earliest memories is of his father placing his revolver in his desk drawer, where the sound of rolling bullets could be heard whenever the drawer was opened or closed. Robert was happy when he was with his father, but it was always a tiring experience because his father liked to walk for miles at a time.

Robert's life at home was not so happy. His mother, Belle, frequently accused her husband of being emotionally abusive toward her because of his drinking. When the time came to have her second child— it was a girl named Jeanie—she took Robert and fled to the East Coast to live with her in-laws until the baby was born. When she returned home, she found her husband in the hospital, where doctors were treating him for consumption, one of the most terrifying diseases of the time.

It took nearly nine years for Will to finally die of the disease. They moved often, because as Will's health deteriorated so did their financial situation. It was a nightmarish situation for a child, but Robert continued to be devoted to his father and accompanied him on his walking rounds, as frightening as they sometimes were. The more Will's health declined, the more determined he became to undertake strenuous physical exercises. For example, he liked to go on twenty-mile hikes and swim in icy ocean waters. Often Will took his son to one of his favorite swimming spots near the San Francisco harbor, where he left Robert behind to guard his clothes and whiskey while he swam a half-mile to a bell buoy.

Robert shook with fear on the beach as he waited for his father to return.

The end came in the spring of 1885, when Robert was eleven years of age. The day before he died, Will went into the newspaper and put in a full day's work. Despite years-long knowledge of his impending death, he left only eight dollars in the bank for his wife and their two children. Fortunately, his parents sent money for them to travel back East, where Belle found work as a schoolteacher.

At first, Belle and the children lived with Will's parents, but that was never a pleasant situation because they sometimes blamed her for not taking better care of Will. They moved when she got a teaching position in another school district. There they found lodgings with Will's sister and her husband, a robust man who served as a healthy role model for Robert, and then later with a Scottish farm couple, where Robert was given work on weekends and after school.

Robert excelled in his academic studies, but his true love was baseball and he dreamt of becoming a professional player. That love of competitive sports was almost certainly a legacy of his father, as was a growing determination to win in whatever competitions he undertook.

Most people would not consider Will a good father, and rightly so— but he compensated for some of his faults by including Robert in his daily activities. Robert learned empathy from his father by observing him interact with other men and by being put in a position in which he had to care for his father. Empathy is an essential ingredient in the making of a poet and Robert possessed it in abundance.

As Robert entered adulthood, he found himself drifting in and out of depression, not uncommon for a son without a father. He suffered from depression for the remainder of his life. Things might have turned out entirely differently for Robert had he not learned, early on, basic survival skills from his father—and had his mother not instinctively known the right things to do after his father's death. By keeping Robert under the influence of positive male role models and encouraging his interest in sports and the arts, she provided him with life-saving guidance—and in the process gave America one of its most beloved poets.

When Robert writes so eloquently of "The Road Not Taken," he speaks for all sons without fathers, and for what might have been:

I shall be telling this with a sigh

Somewhere ages and ages hence:

Two roads diverged in a wood, and I—

I took the one less traveled by,

And that has made all the difference

None of us can say with any certainty what our lives would have been like if our choices had been different, but we can speculate that many sons without fathers would have achieved more, been more gentle, respectful and empathetic, if they had enjoyed relationships with their fathers—that is, if the fathers were capable of being good role models.

All too often, divorced or abandoned mothers feel that the father is the worst influence their son could be exposed to, but they only see the negative aspects of the man's life and usually it has more to do with their personal relationship with the father than it does their son's relationship with him.

Belle Frost apparently had a good heart and was willing to look beyond her conflicts with Robert's father, because she encouraged her son to spend time with his father and to love him. She clearly disapproved of his drinking, but she recognized that, drunk or sober, he still had something to offer their son.

How could Belle put aside her own hurt feelings over the loss of her marriage and still have the strength to allow Will to parent their son?

Belle apparently viewed these as two separate issues. From all accounts, Belle and Will ceased to have a marriage in the traditional sense, but they continued to work together to be good parents. They provide an inspiring example of how devoted parents can reach out to their son, even amid the chaos that characterizes their relationship with each other.

Through the Eyes of a Son

In William Golding's classic novel, *Lord of the Flies*, the story of a group of English schoolboys who are stranded on a deserted island after surviving a plane crash, you cannot help but be drawn to two of the main characters—Ralph, the fair-haired leader of one sub-group of boys, and Piggy, his chubby and bespectacled sidekick.

Early in the story, when the boys were first exploring the island, Ralph and Piggy went swimming in a lagoon. Ralph said he could swim from the time he was five because his father taught him.

"He's a commander in the Navy," he explained. "When he gets leave he'll come and rescue us. What's your father?"

"My dad's dead," Piggy answered, then asked, "When'll your dad rescue us?"

"Soon as he can."

The exchange between Ralph and Piggy points out one of the major differences between a son with a father, due to divorce, and a son without a father, due to death. The latter has a father who doesn't "do anything" and cannot be counted on for even the most mundane of rescues, a father who exists only in the memories of the son.

When a father is lost to divorce, there is always hope that he will return. A father lost to death is lost for all eternity.

Losing a father to death is a painful experience for both mother and son, but it does have some survival advantages for the son, especially if the pre-death family life was happy and the son had a good relationship with the father. Unlike divorce, where old conflicts fester and new ones arise, death offers the son and mother an opportunity to freeze-frame the father in the most flattering light possible.

Dad becomes an idealized parent, especially as the years go by. His picture remains on the wall. Mother becomes misty eyed when she talks about him. That can be good for the son because it gives him someone to look up to and admire, but it can create problems for the mother, who, in the eyes of the son, makes mistakes that the idealized father would have avoided.

"Dad would never punish me for that," goes the refrain.

When the family dream is disrupted by death, it evokes many of the same emotions as divorce. Although the shattered dreams caused by death are often not a result of erosion within the foundation of the marriage, it leaves the surviving spouse feeling hurt and alone. If the marriage offered a good relationship prior to death, some of the hurt can eventually be replaced by loving, comforting memories.

If the marriage was precarious prior to the death, the aftermath may be confusing and worsen the pain caused by feelings of guilt.

When a man is left to parent children alone, friends and family seem to rally around him to offer advice and support. But society seems to assume that when a woman is left alone, she will need financial support rather than parenting assistance—and that is not always the case. The healing process takes on slightly different faces for men and women, but both must find ways to continue on for the children's sake.

Most widows feel anger towards their husbands for leaving them to face parenthood alone. Their issues are very different from those of divorced women, but both must work through the hurt in order to emerge strong enough to carry on. There is a sense of finality with death that helps one to move ahead, whereas with divorce there always seems to be unfinished business. It is not uncommon for divorced women to comment that their hurt would not have been as harsh if they had lost their husband to death instead of divorce.

When a mother has to assume total family responsibilities after the death of her husband she often is overwhelmed and totally unprepared. Although she may have been an independent woman prior to the death, she discovers that the void left by her missing partner is larger than she ever could have imagined, especially when it comes to decisions that must be made about their children. As she tries to move her family forward, she suffers tremendous pain for a very long time.

Scotty's Mom: Love Finds a Way

Scott had a special relationship with his son, Scotty. They went fishing and hiking together, and they played baseball and touch football—all the things that traditionally define the lives of eight-year-old boys. But it wasn't always like that. Before Scott learned that he had inoperable cancer—and had less than a year to live—his relationship with Scotty was purely functional.

Scott and his wife, Annette, had married right out of college, not giving much thought to anything except getting their careers on track—he was in sales and she was in real estate—so it was not until they were about five years into their marriage that they both realized that something was missing in their lives. They decided to have a baby.

When Scotty was born, there were some minor health problems, but nothing that could not be corrected. Annette stayed home with Scotty for eight weeks, then found a nanny for him and returned to work. She resented Scott's decision to return to work the day after Scotty was born, while she stayed at home during those eight weeks; but she kept her thoughts to herself. Instead, she suggested at every opportunity that Scott do things with Scotty on the weekends. Scott did that for about a month, spending each weekend with his son, but it annoyed him that Annette laid out at the pool or visited her friends, while he took Scotty on outings. Shouldn't it be a family affair, he wondered?

The end result was that he backed away from the outings because of the resentment that he felt toward Annette. That only served to increase Annette's resentment toward him because she interpreted his actions as an attack on her child-rearing values. By the time Scotty turned eight, the family operated pretty much on automatic pilot. Everyone went his or her own separate way. Despite the suppressed hostility that Annette and Scott felt toward each other, they seldom had arguments or confrontations.

As happens so often in families, they each reached a separate peace with the things that troubled them—and then carried on as if nothing were wrong. All that came to an end the day Scott came home and told Annette that he had inoperable cancer. She cried. They hugged. Then they sat down on the bed and gazed out the window as if the solution to their problem existed beyond the walls of their home.

"How do we tell Scotty?" Scott asked.

Annette paused for a moment, collecting her thoughts. She patted him gently on the arm and said, "I think you should tell him."

Scott looked at her.

"Me?" he asked. "I think both of us should do it."

"Okay," she answered, sighing.

Scotty was outside tossing his baseball in the air when they called him into the den and asked him to sit between them on the sofa. Scott waited for Annette to begin the conversation, but she merely smiled at him and sat quietly, so he started out by telling Scotty how proud he was of him and how much he loved him.

Finally, with tears rolling down his cheeks, he said, "Son, I've got some bad news."

For Scotty, it was all like something in a video game. Hearing his father tell him about his disease—and about how the doctors had done all they could—was like a scene acted out by animated characters. He listened quietly, surrendering to the moment the way he would do if he had been watching television. When he finished his speech, Scott paused a moment, then asked, "Do you have any questions?"

Scotty shook his head, and Annette hugged him tightly.

After that, Scott spent every spare minute with Scotty. He taught him how to drive the family car and told him how often to change the oil and rotate the tires. He showed him how to drill a hole in a slab of wood. And he explained how his mother would need him to do certain things around the house that she could not do for herself.

Annette found herself in an odd position. Whenever she tried to join the Scott and Scotty party, it was politely suggested to her that she should work on her tan at the pool. She smiled and said, "Oh, boys will be boys," but she deeply resented her exclusion from the group. When she overheard Scott tell Scotty that he would have to help her do things she could not do for herself, she was quietly furious.

Scott's health worsened from month to month, although from all outward appearances, he was perfectly healthy. Since they never discussed Scott's illness again after they broke the news to Scotty, there were times when Scotty forgot all about it and simply reveled in the attention he received from his father.

What Scotty enjoyed the most with his father was accompanying him to get the car serviced. He liked the way the other men at the garage reacted to his dad, like he was important or something. Scott told them jokes and they laughed and told Scotty what a great dad he had. Most adults would have considered the experience mundane, but not Scotty, who reveled in the sounds, sights and odors of those shared experiences.

When the end came, it did not happen the way it does in the movies. Scotty was downstairs, watching television, while his mother prepared breakfast. After a while, she sent him upstairs to awaken Scott for breakfast. Scotty knew something was wrong the moment he entered the bedroom. His dad was stretched out in bed with his eyes vacantly open, as if he were gazing at the ceiling.

"Dad, Mom said breakfast is ready," said Scotty, approaching the bed.

When Scott did not respond, Scotty nudged him with his hand. Nothing. Suddenly, he was overcome with panic. All the way down the staircase, Scotty screamed for his mother, tripping on the final steps and rolling across the carpet into his mother's arms. He pleaded with her to go see about his father, but instead she rushed to the telephone and called 911; then she returned to hold him tightly as the tears flowed.

"Who will be my daddy?" Scotty sobbed.

Scott went to the funeral, but he refused to look inside the casket. Over the next few weeks, he avoided going home after school and found excuses to play with his friends until well after dark. Annette tried to heap attention and affection on him, but he shrugged it off with admonitions that she should leave him alone.

"Mom," he said. "If you loved Dad like I did you'd understand."

Annette led two different lives: In one, she went to work and carried on as she had done before Scott's death; in the other life, she tried to be both mother and father to Scott, and was hurt that he accepted her in neither role. The more she emulated Scott's behavior, the more her son seemed to reject her.

One day she told Scotty to get into the car. She had a surprise for him. To Scotty's horror, she drove to the garage where father and son had enjoyed time together while the car was being serviced. Scotty did not like that at all. The more he withdrew at the garage, the more aggressive Annette became in her efforts to make him feel the old "magic" he had experienced with his father. She struck up conversations with the mechanics. The mechanics were polite to her, but behind her back one of the men winked at his buddies and made an hourglass shape with his hands. Annette did not see that, but Scotty did and it ruined everything special he had shared with his father. It was as if someone had spread oil across the surface of his favorite fishing hole.

In the months ahead, Scotty saw his life change dramatically from what it had been before his father's death. He and his mother moved to an apartment, and that meant he had to change schools. Making new friends was difficult for him under the circumstances, and when the other children found out that he did not have a father, they teased him about it, making his adjustment at school even more difficult. As a result, he avoided participating in any group activities, preferring instead to play with one friend, typically the one who gave him the least amount of grief over not having a father.

Scotty's life changed drastically at the age of twelve, when his mother remarried a man twenty years her senior. The man seemed so settled, so calm about life's annoyances, that she thought he would have a positive influence on Scotty. It didn't work out that way because it turned out that the man's "calmness" was actually a façade for a very rigid approach to life. It was his way—or not at all. The marriage only lasted one year, and both Scotty and his mother were happy to see the man leave.

By the time Scotty turned sixteen, his most distinguishing characteristic was his quick temper. He always seemed to be angry about something. As a result, he spent hours daydreaming about what he was going to do to even the score with his "enemies"—and that list was composed of just about everyone he knew, except his best friend, Robert.

Scotty had no adult males to talk to about the issues that troubled him the most—girls (his mother's only advice was to treat them with respect), bullies (his mother told him to report them to the teacher), sports (his mother liked basketball but hated football), fishing (his mother said she didn't have time), and career goals (his mother suggested he become a doctor). He loved his mother, but it frightened him that he did not have a father to talk to about what he should do with his life. Confused by the flood of emotions he did not understand, he began to focus on the one thing that he knew something about, death. Starting with his dad, he made up lists of all the ways that people could die

One day, he and his friend Robert were riding on his friend's motor scooter, when a gang of their classmates leaped from behind a building and peppered the boys with water balloons, causing Robert to lose control of the scooter. They crashed into a ditch and Robert was knocked unconscious.

Scotty went to the hospital with his friend, expecting the worst, but when the doctors came out and told the family that Robert had passed away, he was devastated. He went straight home and looked for his death list. Nowhere on the list was there a mention of dying from a scooter accident. If he had missed that one, he wondered, what else had he missed? Apparently, no one was safe from death. It could strike at any moment.

That night, after his mother went to sleep, Scotty wrote a long farewell letter that detailed everything he hated about life—beginning with the death of his father and his best friend, and then moving on to the way he felt excluded from activities at school, and then concluding with the happiness he felt over the prospect of seeing his father again.

Then he hanged himself in his closet, using one of his father's belts—or at least he tried to hang himself. Fortunately, his mother heard his frantic kicking against the closet door and ran into his room and cut him down. It was a turning point in their lives. Annette sought professional help for Scotty, and—with the help of an understanding therapist—mother and son were able to reconstruct their family in such a way as to allow them both to work through their problems.

A Common Mistake Moms Make

Scotty may have been depressed for a long time, but after his father's death his life did not spiral out of control because he hated his mother, or because she did not love him, but because events had conspired to deprive him of a lifeline at a time when he needed one the most. It takes more than good intentions to raise a healthy boy. It takes an understanding of how their minds work.

In Scotty's case, the loss of his father was preceded by a purely functional relationship for most of his childhood. Not until his father learned that he was going to die, did he make a major effort to be a father to his son. Scotty was delighted by the new attention he received and quickly forgot the years of substandard parenting he received from his father, which was why he reacted so strongly to the mistakes his mother made when she tried to become a father figure to him.

To Scotty's depressed way of thinking, his mother damaged not only the memory of his father, but also the reality of their mother-son relationship. Instead of building up the remembered relationship Scotty had with his father, she tore down the existing relationship she had with her son by trying to replace his father.

Psychologists once thought that if people who lose loved ones successfully complete the grieving process, going through all its various stages, then they could have a complete recovery. Now we know that's not true for everyone. No matter how successful the grieving process there will always be varying levels of residual pain that must be incorporated into daily living.

It is important for the mothers of sons who have lost their fathers to death to understand that they must both build a new relationship with their son and preserve the positive memory he has of his father. Sometimes that will call for her to walk an emotional tightrope.

The good news, if you can call it that, is that studies have shown that the negative effects of a father's death are not as great as they are for sons who lose fathers for other reasons. That is because children whose fathers have died do not experience the rejection that is associated with other types of loses. If they feel rejection, they are more likely to direct it toward God for taking their father from them.

Sara McLanaham and Gary Sandefur, who have done considerable research on single parents, calculated the chances of dropping out of high school to be 37 percent for children born out of wedlock, 31 percent for children of divorce, and only 15 percent for children whose fathers have died.

That latter figure is interesting because the chances a child in a non-disrupted family will drop out of high school are 13 percent. If that figure is correct—and we have no reason to doubt that it is—it means that of all the things that can go wrong for a son as a result of his father's death, educational problems are not at the top of the list.

That is one way that sons without fathers due to death are different from sons that lost fathers for other reasons: Although all may suffer identical emotional trauma, it has been our experience that sons who lose their fathers to death are better able to maintain an adequate or even superior level of schoolwork.

That is important for a mother to know. First, it lets her know that she cannot use the successful completion of schoolwork as a reliable guide to her son's emotional health. Good grades are not an indication that he is emotionally strong.

Statistically speaking, he will put on a good front in the classroom and carry on as if nothing is wrong, even if he is severely depressed. Second, it gives the mother a foundation upon which to build a better relationship with her son. If her son sees his schoolwork as the stabilizing element in his life, the one thing that keeps him sane, then she can use it to become more involved in his activities. She should talk to him more about his studies, his academic likes and dislikes, his teachers (their strengths and weaknesses), and his goals as an adult. She should ask his opinions about different aspects of the school. By doing those things she can associate herself with the stability that her son finds in schoolwork and encourage him to see common elements of stability in their mother-son relationship.

Despite her best efforts, Scotty's mom raised a son who momentarily lost his way, in part, because she attempted to "mother' male attitudes into him. Her perception of maleness was ad-libbed and based on the assumption that she could teach her son anything that a man could teach him. She did not allow for the possibility that her son had biological and cultural needs that she could not address because of her gender. Equal rights under the law, or in the workplace, do not translate to equal influences as a parent.

Sports Have Their Own Gender Biases

In his book, *Life Without Father*, David Popenoe wrote about what he calls "protest masculinity." It is a phrase that psychologists use to describe the behavior that boys exhibit when they use athletics as a means of breaking away from the dominance of their mothers. In the 1970s, Harvard University researchers Beatrice and John Whiting attributed the break to "an unconscious fear of being feminine."

Some well-meaning authors and therapists have recommended that mothers of sons without fathers assume a male role and engage in sports with their sons. We feel that is one of the most damaging things a mother can do, especially if the father is deceased. Sons who lose their fathers to death or to prison sometimes are bullied by their peers and teased because they do not have a father. For those boys, nothing could be worse than having their mother try to compete with the fathers of their male classmates.

For boys, sports are a refuge from the femininity represented by their mothers. For her to invade that traditionally male territory, especially in the presence of her son's friends, is to subject him to ridicule and self-doubt, emotions that research tells us could lead to abusive behavior toward women later in life.

The fact that his mother may have superior athletic skills to those of his friends' fathers is beside the point. At issue is his fear of becoming like his mother—and anything that she does to aggravate his fears of femininity supersedes any athletic skills she might teach him.

We are not saying that mothers should not play ball with their sons. Any activity that mothers can undertake with their sons is of benefit. If she is athletic, she may even teach him skills that his friends do not have. However, mothers should not consider those activities a substitute for what happens when their sons play ball with older males.

Mothers should remember that the purpose of involving boys in athletics is not to teach them skills that will enable them to win the hearts of homecoming queens, or to someday obtain hefty college scholarships, but to teach them self-control and empathy. A mother may teach her son to throw a perfect curve ball, but she can't teach him the self-control that he will learn from a male coach who shows him how to throw the same pitch. Remember, boys learn by example—they don't learn by explanation. The visual image created by a mother throwing a curve ball does not compute with the son's visual image that he has of himself. Simply put, he does not see himself in his mother.

We Can Learn From Scotty's Close Call

We should not move on from Scotty's life without looking at the bigger picture his story represents. Fatherless children are at dramatically greater risk of suicide.

For young people 15 to 19 years of age, suicide is the third leading cause of death, behind unintentional injury and homicide, claiming an estimated 5,000 lives a year.

For children 5 to 14 years of age, it is the sixth leading cause of death. More teenagers and young adults die from suicide than from cancer, heart disease, AIDS, birth defect, and chronic lung disease combined. Statistically, the numbers associated with child suicide are not significant—about 300 deaths per year for children 10 to 14—but to the families involved it is a devastating experience that affects entire communities. The death of a father—or the absence of a father due to divorce or other causes—figure prominently in suicides among children. According to figures released by Health and Human Services, 63 percent of youth suicides are from fatherless homes.

There are various scenarios for suicide among children, but some of the most common include situations in which divorced parents are severely critical of each other when talking to the child, and when either parent is physically or emotionally abusive to the child. Suicide is also a possibility when sons without fathers develop gender issues as a result of not having a male role model. Some researchers feel that homosexuality is an orientation with a genetic basis. Others feel that homosexuality is a developmental issue that can be manipulated by environment—a position that does not necessarily contradict genetic theorists.

We have no information on the subject beyond what already has been published, but we feel that until such time as the research is conclusive, it is prudent to consider environmental factors, especially the absence of the father in the home, as a possible contributor to gender confusion among some teens. Peer pressure on teens with gender issues is sometimes so overwhelming that suicide becomes an "acceptable" way out for them.

In adolescence, stresses associated with dating can result in suicide. Parents sometimes overlook that possibility because they forget how powerful the emotions and hormones are during adolescence. By the time a boy enters his teens, he is well aware of the sexual potential offered by his female classmates. His strongest emotions are associated with sex. He thinks about sex constantly. He talks about sex with his male friends. And he masturbates when he is alone, sometimes every day.

Early Warning Signs of Suicide

- Change in eating and sleeping habits. Child may overeat or exhibit a loss of appetite. He may sleep too much or complain of not sleeping enough. He may decline to eat his favorite food.

- Loss of energy (may or may not be clearly related to sleep loss). He may say that he is "too tired" to go to the store.

- Withdrawal from family activities and time spent with friends, accompanied by an increase in time spent watching television or playing video games.

- Drug or alcohol use.

- Unexplained drop-off of work habits at school (an A student suddenly becomes a D student).

- A series of physical complaints, such as headache, stomachache, etc. Pay attention if he says he "feels bad" but can't explain where it hurts.

- Aggressive behavior against family members, friends, pets or himself.

- A romance gone bad. Parents should not underestimate the emotional trauma their teen or pre-teenage son can experience over unrequited "puppy love."

- Mysterious comments, such as "What's the point," or "I won't be a problem for you much longer."

Sons without fathers often feel cheated because they mistakenly think that their other male friends, at least those who have fathers, know more about sex than they do because they have fathers who can instruct them. That's not the case, but since boys rarely discuss such things with each other, sons without fathers assume that they have been short-changed on all matters dealing with sex.

Once a boy sets his sights on a girl, the courtship process can build over a period of months, even years. If, after months or years of anguish, the boy finally summons the courage to approach the girl, a rejection can be so devastating as to make life seem as if it is no longer worth living. If the boy is an Unfriendly World child, suicide can appear to be a reasonable way out of his pain, for he will assume that the world is so unfriendly as to never allow him to experience love or sex.

CHAPTER 4

Problem Areas Where Parents Can Make a Difference

Already feeling hurt and at a higher risk for school failure, a son without a father can only sink lower when he can't achieve to expectation. A learning disorder is an added curse. Many learning problems are not recognized until the child has experienced significant failure. Teachers and parents may blame the child for not trying hard enough, not paying attention or not listening before they realize there is a real problem.

When a learning problem is identified, mothers need to be persistent in dealing with the school in getting assistance for their sons. They have a responsibility to fully understand the problems and work together with the school in developing a reasonable educational plan.

If that is not possible they should volunteer to work with the child at home on extra activities. Mothers should help the child focus and use his strengths to help overcome his weaknesses. Parental assistance may include the following:

- Helping him organize his homework
- Providing a structured and predictable home environment
- Telling him what you want, not what you don't want.
- Helping him learn from his mistakes
- Stressing accuracy, not speed.
- Playing games that encourage him to learn.
- Offering rewards when he does well.

When a mom tells her son that he is "just like his father," she usually has one of two things in mind: She either wants to encourage him or place blame for his failures. No matter what the intention, whether positive or negative, it does go to the core of father-son relationships. Boys imitate their fathers. There is nothing better for a boy than to have a good male role model. By watching a father conform to the rules of society, set and achieve goals, experience failure and exercise self-control, a son has a roadmap to follow.

Mothers should encourage absent fathers to take the time to help with homework, join a parent's organization, attend school activities, talk to the teachers, and understand his child's learning strengths and weaknesses. When a loving dad is willing to confess weaknesses to his son, it usually strengthens the innate bond between them. If the son considers his dad to be successful, he will probably be surprised to hear any admission of past weaknesses. A beneficial conversation between a father and a son might go something like this:

> **You are so much like me. I was never good in reading or spelling, so I concentrated on math, which was my strong subject. Now, in my job, I don't have to read aloud or fast. I seldom have many pages to comprehend at once. It helps that I'm a good listener and I have an excellent memory. I dictate all my correspondence and seldom even have a need to pick up a pen. Son, I know it's really tough right now for you, but someday you'll find the right career that matches your strengths.**

In general, young boys have more difficulty than girls paying attention in school, carrying out school assignments, and being conscientious in their work. They are slightly more immature during those critical elementary years than girls. Having a father involved in the learning process makes a difference. Research shows that boys perform better and have fewer discipline problems in the school and community when their fathers are actively involved in their life.

Obtaining dad's involvement, by whatever methods works, will pay dividends to both mother and son. Not all sons can be high achievers in school, but most can gain the necessary basics to accomplish their life dreams and become productive citizens.

Sobering Educational Facts

Children from fatherless homes are twice as likely to drop out of school, according to the U.S. Department of Health and Human Services. Other government research shows that children from father-absent homes have lower IQ's and lower verbal and performance scores, with males being more affected.

Fatherless boys achieve at a lower level than girls in all academic areas, particularly in reading and writing, but paternal deprivation puts them at a distinct disadvantage in math, a subject that has been clearly linked to paternal involvement.

In general, the presence of a father in the child's life has greater impact on educational achievement than race, social class or gender, beginning in early elementary school. The National Principal's Association reports that 71 percent of all high school dropouts come from fatherless homes.

Female vs. Male Teachers
Do the Math

To better understand your school-age son, you need to look at his world through his eyes. He is in your care for sixteen hours or so each day—less if you are a working mother, which is almost always going to be the case with sons without fathers.

But that calculation is misleading since he will be asleep, hopefully, during half of that time. That leaves you with, say, four to eight hours a day to actually influence his life, depending on whether you work and have him in day care, in which case you would be lucky to spend two to four hours a day with him.

Do the math. On a daily basis, your son's teachers spend more time with him than you can ever hope to do. If you bring work home from the office, or if you pursue an active social life, then that four-to-eight potential hours a day is from time to time reduced to nothing more than a friendly, "good night."

With that in mind, if your son's teachers are all women, what chance does he have to forge a strong male identity? Men make up only 10 percent of elementary teachers and only 40 percent of high school teachers. Your son could go for years at a stretch in elementary school without having a male teacher. Those are not acceptable odds for a son without a father.

If your son is African American or Hispanic, he could go through twelve years of schooling without ever coming face to face with a teacher that looks like him. According to 1999-2000 census figures, only 7.6 percent of teachers are black and only 5.6 percent are Hispanic (break those figures down by gender and it is apparent that, statistically speaking, black or Hispanic male teachers are almost non-existent).

Reg Weaver, the 2003 president of the National Education Association, told *USA Today* that the "sad reality is that a young boy could go through his entire education without ever having a teacher who looks like me." Weaver, who is black, said that the demand for male teachers of all races is high in public schools across America.

With odds like that, what chance does a black or Hispanic son without a father have to avoid the problems associated with the Unfriendly World Syndrome if his mother has a full-time job and makes no effort to find male role models for him?

The gender imbalance in the classroom has been referred to by some as feminization, but we do not like that term because it implies a deliberate or conscious effort by women to improperly program boys' minds. That's simply not the case. Women dominate education because that has been one of the few fields open to them over the years and because men have been more attracted to higher paying professions.

Aside from the role-model issue, female dominance in the classroom is bad for boys because studies have shown that female teachers tend to reward "feminine" behavior in boys (sitting quietly and exhibiting non-assertive behavior) and they tend to punish boys for being aggressive in the classroom or on the playground during recess. They tend to give girls higher grades, even when the work product is of equal quality (probably because the girl's work is neater). And they tend to spend more time answering questions asked by girls. These biases are not intentional, but they are predictable.

Our advice to mothers is simple: Become an activist for your son's cause. You have more power than you think. Schedule time with the principle and ask if there is anything that he or she can do to help your son have more male teachers. If the response is that there are simply not enough male teachers to go around, suggest that the principal re-think the classroom assignments and deliberately assign sons without fathers to male teachers. Use this book to bolster your argument that your request is reasonable.

If you are unable to persuade your son's principal of the merits of a policy change, then attend the next school board meeting and make your case. Tell the board members that the school is not addressing your son's needs and you have suggestions for how to make needed changes. Repeat the suggestion you made to the principal and recommend that the board go one step further and make an effort to recruit more male teachers at both elementary and high-school levels. Do the things that your son's female teachers do not want him to do—be assertive and don't take no for an answer.

Dealing with Hazing and Bullying

The children of divorced fathers, or those who have been abandoned, are often immune to taunts from their peers, unless they are distinctive for some other reason, such as physical handicaps, birth deformities, racial or cultural differences, or because they are intellectually gifted and make their peers feel inadequate.

That immunity is granted because so many children today fall in that category. That is not always the case for sons whose fathers have died or gone to prison. Although it appears to be a cruel twist of misguided fate, one of the more ominous things that boys who have lost their fathers to death or prison must contend with when they return to school are taunts and bullying from their male classmates.

Eight-year-old Edward was devastated by the imprisonment of his father after his conviction for involuntary manslaughter related to an automobile accident. One day his father was playing ball with him in the back yard. The next day he was handcuffed and taken off to prison. His mother told him that his father would not come home for twenty years. Edward counted on his fingers: he would be twenty-eight before his daddy came home again!

On his first day back at school the teachers made it a point to be nice to him. They spoke to him in the hallway, making his name sound special. They asked him how he was "doing," but they didn't wait around for an answer. Edward's classmates were different. They fell into three distinct groups—those who avoided eye contact and conversation with him; those who interacted with him, but acted as if nothing had happened; and those who tormented him on the playground. It was that latter group that made his time at school a living hell.

"Edward's daddy is a jailbird!" taunted one chubby boy who followed him around on the playground, broadcasting that fact to anyone who would listen. Each time Edward insisted that he stop, the larger boy pushed him to the ground.

Edward didn't fight back because his mother had made him promise never to fight—and, with the loss of his father, it seemed even more important to obey his mother.

"What if my mother died?" he thought. "What would I do then?"

Within days, it became great sport at school for the male students to tease him about his father. It was like those *National Geographic* specials on television when wounded animals are attacked by their own kind. Once he was walking down the hall, when a boy he did not know well ran up behind him and tripped him, sending him tumbling to hard floor. Taunted the boy, "Why don't you ask you daddy to help you up?"

Several other students gathered around, looking down at him on the floor as if he were road kill. Then the sing-song chanting began: "Edward's daddy is a jailbird! Edward's daddy is a jailbird! Edward's daddy is a jailbird!"

One day in class a teacher handed out permission slips for a field trip. "Just ask your fathers to sign it," she said. A little girl sitting on the front row looked horrified. "What's Edward going to do," she asked. "He doesn't have a daddy!"

With that the entire class stirred and buzzed with confusion.

Not long after that the school principal stopped by the office where Edward's mother worked and asked if he could have a few words in private with her. He told her about the hazing that Edward was experiencing at school and explained that he was hesitant to intervene, for fear that it would only prolong the taunts.

Edward's mother was shocked. He had said nothing about his difficulties at school. She had noticed that he was more withdrawn than usual, but she thought that was probably because he missed his father.

"What am I supposed to do?" she asked.

The principal looked uncomfortable.

"Someone told me that you made him promise not to fight. Is that correct?"

"Yes," she answered.

"You didn't hear this from me—and I'll swear I never said it—but I don't think Edward's problems are going to go away until he defends himself. They see his reluctance to fight as a weakness."

"Did I hear you right? You want me to tell him to fight?"

The principal looked uneasy, as if he were participating in an illegal transaction and was concerned about being caught.

"Like it said, I never said it. But I do think that if Edward's father were here, he would tell him to protect himself, even if it meant fighting."

That afternoon, when Edward came home from school, his mother told him that she understood that he was having problems at school.

"Remember when I asked you to promise me that you would never fight?"

Edward nodded.

"Well, I'm not going to hold you to that anymore. I don't want to ever hear of you picking a fight, but you have my permission to fight back if someone hits you or trips you."

"Really!" said Edward, his eyes bulging.

"Really."

The next day Edward was again accosted by the chubby boy, who dispensed with the taunting foreplay and slugged him on the shoulder, knocking him to the ground. Said the chubby boy, "Why don't you just call your daddy?"

Without another word, Edward jumped to his feet and tore into the chubby boy, punching him in the face with rights and lefts, until the boy fell to the ground, his face bloody and bruised. To Edward's surprise, the chubby boy struggled to come to his feet, and then broke into a run, jumbo tears streaming down his cheeks.

Watching from a distance was the principal. Once he saw the outcome, he turned and walked away, a secretive smile betraying his pleasure at the sudden turn of events. Within days, the playground balance of power shifted. Edward became a hero to the other children who also had been bullied by the chubby boy. Not surprisingly, his chief antagonist soon became his best friend, a fairly common occurrence in those situations.

We don't recommend that principals, teachers and parents instruct their children to use violence to solve their problems, but we do think it would be a good idea for the parents of school-age children who are being bullied to arrange for them to receive instruction in marital arts, whether it is judo, karate, wrestling or boxing, with a clear understanding that the skills they learn will be used only for self-defense.

Actually, it is rare for boys who are trained in self-defense to become bullies themselves. That's because bullies are children who have self-image problems. Perhaps they are overweight, like Edward's tormentor, or perhaps they simply do not have academic skills that would allow them to stand out among their peers. Or perhaps they are experiencing anxiety because of problems at home. Whatever the reasons, bullies act out physically and verbally in an attempt to have power over those they consider more fortunate or those they perceive to be weaker.

Children that have been trained in self-defense typically have a higher self-image than their classmates because they learn skills that others do not know and because they feel more confident about their ability to survive on the playground. They are not likely to suddenly become bullies simply because they have the skills to do so. Actually, instead of teachers punishing bullies—actions that always make the situation worse—it might be more beneficial to require them to participate in marital arts programs if the goal is to eradicate the root cause of the bullying. If you build up their self-image, you tear down the fears and insecurities that made them into bullies in the first place.

Hazing and bullying are major problems in schools today, even for boys who have fathers. One study found that one in five students is bullied at school at least once a week. Such hazing runs the gambit from verbal abuse to beatings, to being urinated upon, to violent sexual abuse, usually with sticks or other implements. Girls are not immune to hazing, but boys are the main targets, primarily because hazing has been viewed over the years as a form of male bonding. The thinking is, "I went through it, so you should, too."

If your son is being bullied at school, we recommend that you do the following:

* Enroll him in martial-arts training. There is nothing wrong with teaching your son to defend himself. Civilization is based on the deeply held cultural belief that self-defense is justified by events that are beyond one's control. It is never wrong for your son to defend himself against physical abuse.

* Meet with your son's teachers and principal. Explain to them what has been happening (in most cases they will already be aware

of it). Ask them to work with you in devising a plan to help your son. If their response is to say that if they punish the bully they are afraid it will only make matters worse, then suggest that they take the opposite strategy and reward the bully whenever he does anything right. They could give him assignments—raising or lowering the flag, for example—and then praise him when he does it correctly. It may seem counter-intuitive to reward someone who has behaved badly, but when you praise him for doing something right you go to the heart of the problem by raising the bully's self-esteem.

* Talk to your son about ways to deflect the teasing and bullying he experiences at school. Talk to him about the verbal taunts, if indeed he will tell you about them, and give him appropriate non-hostile responses, preferably of a humorous nature. Help him make friends with the "cool" guys in his school by inviting them on special outings under the supervision of a male role model. Don't supervise the outings yourself, since that will only expose your son to more teasing.

* If none of the above works—and if your son attends a large school—consider enrolling him in a smaller school where individual students will receive more attention. The smaller the school, the more difficult it is for a bully to mark off his territory.

Sons Want to be Respected

A mother ransacks her teenage son's bedroom in a search for illegal drugs. She explains it to him with the phrase, "I did it because I love you." To her, there is no greater expression of caring than to do something out of love.

Unfortunately, the son does not see it that way. To him, there is no greater expression of caring than showing respect. He doesn't want to bargain for her love because he figures she already owes him that. He never asked to be born. What he wants most in life is to be respected by his mother and his peers.

When you violate his private space, for whatever reason, you disrespect him as a male. **Fathers want to be respected and mothers want to be loved**. Sons seem to instinctively understand that concept and they base all their relationships on it.

That is where Scotty's mom crossed the line. When she took him to the garage that he had gone to with his dad—and unknowingly was treated with disrespect by winking mechanics—she put her son in an impossible situation. He was not large enough to protect her from the mechanics—and, even if he were large enough, the prospect of defending his mother, even if only with words, at the expense of the relationship he and his father had built with the mechanics seemed unfair to him.

When Scotty's mother volunteered to help the football coach during practice she invited the criticism of his peers, who showed the ultimate disrespect by making sexual comments about her perceived relationship with the coach. By showing disrespect to her, they showed disrespect to Scotty. He did not blame his friends; he blamed his mother for putting him in a vulnerable position. She should have known better. Mothers should worry less about whether their sons love them and worry more about whether they respect them. That may seem harsh, but adolescence is a harsh experience for all involved. When a son loses his father, he loses his lifeline to masculine respect. The best way to help your son deal with that loss is to avoid hurting him further with your behavior. Statements of love mean nothing to a teenage boy: he judges your love by your actions, not by what you say. If your son is having respect issues with you, there are certain accusations that will keep popping up in conversation:

> * "Mom, you don't listen to a word I'm saying!"
> * "Why don't you respect my privacy?"
> * "Why don't you ever ask my opinion?"
> * "Please don't embarrass me in front of my friends."

Mothers can avoid some of those problems by considering the effect of their actions on their son. Sure, you have a right to be friendly with any man you choose, but if it is a man who has a relationship with your son and his friends, you can be certain that it will negatively impact your relationship with your son.

If you suspect that your son is experimenting with drugs—or entertaining thoughts of suicide—you have an obligation to go through his things. Just be sure you know what you are looking for: plastic bags or wrappers with a residue of a substance that looks like tobacco, or exotic looking pipes (marijuana); vials that contain a white powder or small white rocks (cocaine and crack); pills that are not in prescription bottles (could be anything from tranquilizers to amphetamines); metal spoons, hypodermic needles and plastic tubing (heroin); and rubber baby-bottle nipples (used to bite down on while taking ecstasy, or used to take crack cocaine). If you find any of the above, you need to confront your son, privacy issues aside, and then seek professional help.

Whether you find drugs or not, you are likely to find pornography, so once you go down that road be prepared for that outcome. We do not recommend that you make an issue of it or even acknowledge it.

Masturbation is a common practice for teenage boys. They all do it, some more so than others. If you make a big deal out of finding pornography in your son's room, it will create huge respect issues with him without changing his behavior. He will continue to masturbate, no matter how much you punish him or embarrass him. However, if he is blatant in his fascination with pornography, to the extent of leaving magazines or pictures out where you will easily find them, then you have no choice but to confront him since the issue may not be masturbation. It may be an attempt on his part to force the respect issue with you, or it may be a sign that he has other serious issues with you.

Little Man of the House

In a single-parent household all the family responsibilities and decisions are thrust on one parent, usually the woman. Having to manage every aspect of family life alone is made worse when there is no contact with the father. Sometimes, because of extreme anger with the father, some women forgo his help in order to keep him out of their life. In extreme cases, women give up child support in exchange for no contact.

In single-parent homes, the children assume more responsibility than if there were two parents available. Separation, divorce, death or prison can modify everyone's daily activities. Working mothers often find themselves overwhelmed by financial pressures, and maintaining the home, not to mention the behavioral issues associated with the kids.

In the event of divorce, a single mother sometimes will be unhappier than she was before the divorce. She becomes irritable and has no interest in activities she once found pleasurable. She eats too much, or too little. She has a low energy level and a general feeling of sadness. Even so, she is usually steadfast in proclaiming that she is better off without the father in the home.

In the midst of trying to carry the load of the whole family, feeling isolated and uninterested in sharing with others, single mothers often turn to their children. Evidence indicates that children of single parents mature more quickly, are exposed to more adult situations, and participate more in family decisions.

In stressful times, single mothers tend to draw the family inward, sharing their pain and family responsibilities more. They may explain to the children that without the father everyone will have to help out more. Depending on the level of dysfunction, the mother is likely to turn to the oldest child to assume the "other parent" role. In those situations, not only does the child help make family decisions, he often becomes the mother's closest companion.

When a mother turns to her daughter for support, the pair becomes peers or friends. They talk long hours about the trials of life. The mother seems to regress somewhat as the daughter matures a bit. Often the pair spends time together, as if they were the same age. Typically, the daughter neglects her needs in order to meet her mother's emotional needs. The end result can be less than amiable.

Some daughters resent the mom's interference in her social circle; she may be jealous of her mom's ability to be the center of attention among her friends, and she may want her mother to seek her own friends.

Others may mature quickly and begin to circulate more in the adult social circles. Many actually compete with their mother for male attention. On those occasions when the single mom initiates her son as the "other parent," that relationship is usually very different from a mother-daughter parenting pair. The son is vulnerable in a family where there is no father figure. He feels the tension of his mother's depression and her neediness. Sensing that his mother is emotionally fragile, he takes on a companionship role because he feels responsible for her.

A son without a father already sees the world as an unfriendly place, so when he realizes that his mother is suffering too, that only intensifies his belief about the world. He may assume more and more household responsibilities. He may offer advice to his mother and check on her frequently. The son begins not only to take on extra duties to relieve his mother's load, but he may actually start guiding her through her life changes. He soon becomes the father to the other siblings, disciplinarian and the spokesman for the family. He baby-sits, cleans, cooks and keeps the household on track. He is the one who greets guests at their front door.

In these situations, the mother usually is too dysfunctional to comprehend how damaging this arrangement is for her son. Instead of caring and protecting the son, she allows a role reversal so that it is she who is being cared for. Over time, the mother's dependency can grow into a very problematic situation.

A mother that is dependant on her son can become very comfortable going to the movies with him, playing tennis with him, attending community activities with him, and even attending parent-teacher conferences concerning the younger siblings. He is encouraged to be strong, reliable and responsible for the other family members. He feels needed and enjoys the power of his role, while feeling powerless in the overall world. His self-image is superficially enhanced by this leadership role. At times he is expected to actually take control and tell his mother what to do. He is involved in the financial decisions and seems to have equal say in family decisions.

The son that finds himself in that position typically builds anger and resentment. Although he feels powerful in his new role, there is a part of him that feels hurt that he has been called upon to sacrifice his youth. At some point, he begins to realize that he is actually helping or stepping in for his father. He slowly starts to understand that he is really his mother's second choice—and that causes anger toward her.

After serving as a pseudo-parent—and sharing many of the important family decisions—sons do not return to the child role easily. Sometimes, when the mother starts dating and sharing decision-making tasks with another adult male, the son becomes very confused. After being forced to mature too quickly, he becomes alienated from his peers. If a mother sends him back to child status again, it often is more than he can handle.

We advise mothers to resist the temptation to allow their sons to become surrogate husbands. There is basically no way that situation can have a happy ending for either the mother or the son. The best thing that a mother can do for her son is to be alert to the type and amount of family responsibility she allows him to assume. Encourage him to help out around the house, but draw the line at sharing family financial information or sharing personal fears that will make it necessary for him to be the comforter.

Lastly, mothers should remember that being the "Little Man" of the house initially has a positive ring to a son who is flattered to be referred to as a man, but it eventually loses its appeal when the son realizes that the operative word in that phrase is "little."

CHAPTER 5

Chasing After Phantom Fathers

Southern novelist Harry Crews was twenty-one months old when his father died of a heart attack. Crew's concept of his relationship with his father was complicated by his mother's remarriage shortly after his father's death.

For her second husband, Crews' mother chose his father's brother, a fact she never bothered to explain to Crews. Not knowing any better, he grew up calling his new father "Daddy." He loved the man dearly, all the more so because he found the smell of whiskey on his breath pleasant, sweeter scented even than the soap with which he bathed. It baffled him that his sweet smell was such a source of discord in the home, with his mother constantly telling him that he was going "kill himself and ruin everything" if he continued to drink.

Crews' mother and stepfather fought often, he later recalled in his splendid, yet heart-breaking, autobiography, A Childhood: The Biography of a Place. Their last fight, the one that sealed the fate of the marriage—and, by effect, doomed the family—was indelibly stamped in his young memory. His stepfather came into his bedroom, where he was already in bed, having heard every word of what amounted to a five-hour fight between his mother and stepfather.

"I ain't gone be by to see you no more," the father said.

"Never?"

The father explained that he couldn't see him any more because Crews' mother had a "peace bond" out on him.

Crews was confused.

"I never was your daddy, but I tried to be one to you. It just wasn't in me though."

Crews felt a burning sensation running up and down his nerves. *Was not my daddy? Not my daddy? Is that what I heard?*

Shocked, Crews asked him who his father was.

"My brother," he answered.

Years later, after he had served a stint in the Marine Corps and enrolled as a student at the University of Florida, Crews decided to look up the man he had grown up thinking was his "Daddy." The meeting did not go well. "He was sitting in the back of a tiny store, huddled beside a stove in a huge overcoat," Crews recalled. "He was very nervous. He did not want to talk. I left minutes after I got there. We never touched each other, not even to shake hands."

As an adult, Crews set out to find his father. He later wrote, "I've always thought that because my daddy died before I could ever know him, he became a more formidable memory, a greater influence, and a more palpable presence than he would ever have been had he lived. I'm not sure precisely what that says about me, but surely it must say more about me than it does about my daddy or his death."

It would be fair to say that Crews became obsessed with re-constructing a believable image of his birth father, but that obsession was probably no stronger than it is for any other son without a father. He discovered that his father, at six feet two, was tall—taller than he would ever grow to be—and possessed great energy for whatever undertaking he attempted, and "already had enough trouble and sickness and loss in his short life to have broken a lesser man."

The problem with a son re-constructing his father from the stories of others who knew him is that invariably they recall only the best and the worst—and isn't most of life lived in between? His father becomes either larger than life, a veritable deity, or lower than life, almost to the level of an affable reptile.

By the time Crews met Sally Ellis, the woman of his dreams, he was committed to becoming a writer (if for no other reason than to sort out his childhood). They married in 1960, when Crews was twenty-five and *still in college—and nine months later they had a son, whom they named Patrick Scott. Crews taught junior high English for a time, but then returned to school to pursue a master's degree in English.*

While he was still attending graduate school, they filed for divorce. No surprise there. Sons without fathers typically find marriage rough going, especially if they have unresolved issues with their fathers (or step-fathers). Sally took Patrick and moved out of the state. Without meaning to, Crews had made his own son a son without a father, something that must have resonated somewhere in his thoughts or dreams, for he pursued a reconciliation with Sally "out of love and longing for my son" that ended in them marrying for a second time. As a result, their second son, Byron Jason, was born in 1963. At that point, it looked like a happy ending to a sad story.

Then tragedy struck. Crews was sleeping in one morning, after writing late into the night, when he was awakened by Sally's screams, broken sentences that alerted him that Patrick was in danger. He jumped out of bed, rushed outside and followed Sally's instructions to the neighbor's swimming pool, where Patrick was face down in the water at the deep end. Crews tried to save his son's life, but it was too late.

Patrick's death was too much for their marriage to absorb, so Crews and Sally divorced for a second time, thus making Byron Jason a son without a father. In an essay titled "Fathers, Sons, Blood," Crews wrote, "I picked up a magazine not long ago in which a man was writing about his children. In the very beginning of the piece, he said, 'The storms of childhood and adolescence had faded into the past.' He would be the poorer for it if that were true. But it is not true, not for him or for any father. The storms don't fade into the past, nor do all the moments that are beautiful and full of happiness."

Crews's obsession with reconstructing his phantom father is no different than millions of others. Sons that never knew their fathers have such a profound need for a father that they will go to any length to reconstruct him out of whatever materials are available. Phantom fathers inhabit the planet in ever increasing numbers, voiceless reminders of the power of the father-son bond, however imperfect.

When Father Was Never There

Definitions of fatherhood can range all the way from simply supplying the biological material for the fertilization of a female egg, a simple act on the male's part, to engaging in a lifelong commitment to love and support a child.

Some men take the first step, but for a variety of reasons, falter on seeing it through. Reasons can vary as much as the personalities involved.

Homes with fatherless children are not always the father's fault. Men can be eliminated from the family unit due to death, divorce, prison, pregnancy through sperm banks, or pregnancies never revealed to the father. But, for whatever reason, when a man's contribution to fatherhood is only biological, everyone is affected.

Many sons waste valuable time during their early years, hoping and imagining that the phantom father they have created in their minds will be their key to happiness. The fantasy of "what if" sometimes interferes with what loving mothers have to offer.

For some sons, the obsession with a phantom father prevents what otherwise could be a productive, happy life. They believe that their dad would have been a totally involved, loving father had he been in the home. They fantasize about happy interactions, exciting outings, and shared dreams. They ignore any evidence to the contrary, even when many of their friends have fathers in the home, but lack the desired happiness. The dream that "my dad would have been different" persists.

Parenting From the Grave

When a father dies, sons sometimes elevate him to a god-like status. No matter what the facts may be—he may have been public enemy number one—the son will never be convinced that he was anything other than a great man. We feel that it is not important to try to force the son to accept negative information about a man he can never confront.

When the death was caused by the father's own bad choices, such as drug use or other risky behavior, the mother is better off separating the behavior from the person. A son innately wants to love his absent father and his mother needs to respect that. Criticism of the deceased man will only worsen an already difficult situation.

It is more productive to use the deceased dad as a motivator for achievement and good behavior, rather than criticizing him and comparing the son to his father when he misbehaves. Comments about how his deceased father would have been proud of him in times of success will go much farther in changing the son's bad behavior.

Most people are much more forgiving of the dead than they are of the living. A mom who is left all alone to provide the discipline, care and love for the family, to make all the decisions and to pay all the bills, often may experience pangs of jealousy of the deceased. The father, whether it is his fault or not, is permanently relieved of his parental responsibilities and somehow forgiven by the son for any mistakes in life.

By default, the remaining parent is suddenly expected to assume double duty for raising the children, with no hope of ever having support and assistance from the biological father. Family and friends sometimes expect the mother to continue on with unprecedented heroic strength. Sometimes mothers find it tempting to compete with the deceased father, but no matter how difficult life becomes for her, she must resist, because if she succumbs to that temptation, she is only insuring long-term conflicts with her son.

Who Made Him Leave?

When divorce occurs prior to father/son bonding, the family dynamics are tainted by the son's unfulfilled dreams of how wonderful life would have been had his father not left. The hurt and anger of the son is seldom left unexpressed. When he doesn't get the answers he wants to hear, he fills in the blank spaces of his family history with stories that protect him from feeling unlovable.

A son without a father must resolve the "whys" and "what ifs" in a way that he can live with. He quickly develops a philosophy that "the world is an unfriendly place" to be survived rather than enjoyed. Most often, the son sacrifices closeness with his mother in order to create a fictional connection with the missing father. Within his Unfriendly World belief system, it is reasonable for the son to believe that his mother is somehow at fault—or, even worse, that he somehow helped drive the father away.

Mothers must not only deal with a son's misplaced anger and frustration, they also must try to teach him to take responsibility for his behavior. In doing that, it is easy to use the absent father as an example of irresponsibility. Many mothers prefer that their ex-spouse stay completely away from the son and family. Those feelings are usually the products of self-protection, not maliciousness.

Our court system sets families up for failure. So many divorce courts place the mother in charge of the family and award visitation for the father on week-ends and holidays. She must handle all the daily tasks of managing the family, while the father goes about his daily life during the week and then shows up for an entertaining week-end.

Children come home from visiting their father bragging that they spent the past two days buying toys, going to the movies and playing. The father doesn't have to help with homework, take off from work when the children are sick, or be consistently firm but loving in disciplinary challenges. Fathers often claim that there are few behavior problems when they have the children. Of course, there are few problems when a father makes no demands on the children, has no limits on buying gifts, and puts no limits on what they eat, usually taking them to fast food places for their favorite treats. He has limited time with them and understandably wants everything to be pleasant.

The most damaging thing that a mother can ever do to her son is to tell him that his father is "not worth loving." Saying it may give her satisfaction, but it may alienate her son from her in ways she can't imagine.

In situations in which there are "good guy/bad guy" roles for parents, it is inevitable that there will be winners and losers. Mothers lose because they are so hurt, angry, and stressed over doing it all alone, while the father only carries the financial burden without other responsibilities. They understandably criticize the father. They find themselves frequently complaining about his lack of interest in the children's emotional needs. As the son hears the criticism, he builds a protective wall around himself, not believing that his father could be at fault. The father also loses, often without knowing it. He is unable to make the contributions that only a father can make to a son.

Often he neglects to teach him the skills of life. He doesn't let him "hang out" with him, go on errands, be around other men, learn how to interact with others in a masculine way, and respect women. The effects of a father's loss may not be evident as early as the mother's loss, but they clearly impact a son's life just as much.

Austin's Quest for His Father

Austin and Jennifer wanted to work out their marital problems, but his temper outbursts were tearing the family apart. He had been raised without a father and he desperately wanted to keep his family together and be a good father to his son, Andrew. Austin readily admitted that he had a bad temper, but he maintained that he only lost his cool when provoked by others. In other words, it was never his fault.

Jennifer felt that she never pleased Austin. No matter what she did, he always found fault with her and their son. She felt that Austin had difficulty being happy unless he was in total control. He demanded perfection of everyone, and with the slightest mistake, he exploded with harsh, hurtful words and threats. Afterwards he would justify his outbursts, blame others, and sheepishly remind his family that he said things when angry that he didn't really mean.

In his second therapy session with us, Austin was asked to tell us about his father. "Throughout my childhood, I never met my father," he said. "Until age twenty-one, I had never seen him, spoken to him, played a game with him, or shared a meal with him. He existed only in my imagination, so I imagined the best. I felt like if I didn't pretend that my father is a wonderful man who really loved me and wanted to be with me, I would lose all hope—I imagined the best, until I actually met him and saw the worst."

With that, Austin changed the subject and talked about his mother, Frances. He acknowledged putting his mother through torture, blaming her for his fatherless home. Without being told much about his father, he created his own life story, imagining that she had forced him to leave and denied him access to his son. In his pain, Austin concluded that she was so jealous of his father that she lied about who he was and why he was not with them. The truth was that his mother never said much about his father.

Austin wanted to be with a man he had never met, while being constantly angry with a woman that was not at fault for his father's absence. For twenty-four years, she endured Austin's misplaced wrath over his "phantom father," while concentrating on her two jobs to make ends meet. She knew that Austin's phantom father was perfect in her son's eyes, but she had no way of knowing how painful his presence was felt by her son, even though—as with all phantom pain—there was no reality to his existence.

Austin saw the world as an unfriendly place where bad things happen and young boys are denied their fathers. Austin's world was a place where he had to endure the pain of not having a father involved in his life. He never had a father in the stadium during ball games. He never went camping with his dad, nor did he have a father to teach him to fish or hunt. The most devastating blow came when he was chosen "player of the week" at his last football game during his senior year of high school and his mom could not attend due to work. For years he couldn't forgive her.

As the therapy session with Austin continued, he had to be confronted and re-directed to discuss his father. He started out by describing him with strong curse words; then he somberly said, "After all

94

those years of me making up excuses—he never wanted me in the first place."

Austin's father had not told Frances that he was dating other girls when he went off to college on a football scholarship. The summer before she was to join him at the university, she found out that she was pregnant. Although Frances was upset by the news, she had no doubt that he would marry her. She believed in their love with all her heart and she was devastated by his insistence that she should have an abortion. If they got married, he explained, he would loose his scholarship. When she refused to have an abortion, he said terrible things about her, and accused her of being unfaithful to him. Finally, he denied that the baby was even his child.

In her guilt and shame over becoming pregnant, Austin's mother moved away from their hometown and had nothing more to do with his father. She was determined to provide for her child without asking for help. Austin's father always knew how to find them, but never did.

At age twenty-one, Austin convinced his aunt to give him enough information to locate his father. After making an appointment with him in a fictitious name, Austin entered a towering office plaza and headed for the eighteenth floor, which overlooked the state capitol. His pride swelled as he sat in a palatial waiting room. Framed degrees lined the wall, and from the looks of the office, his dad appeared very successful.

Thoughts swirled through his mind. *Will he be excited to meet me? Will he want to meet my wife and son? How will he feel about being a grandfather?* As Austin entered his father's office, he was amazed at their resemblance. He felt like he was looking into a mirror. His father was as handsome as he had imagined.

He, too, must have played football in his day, he thought, as he grinned from ear to ear. Introducing himself only as Austin, he shook hands and took a seat in a chair across the desk from him. His father greeted him in an authoritative voice that demanded attention. It was clear that he had the same determination that his son possessed.

"What can I do for you, son?" he asked.

Austin's heart skipped a beat at the mere mention of the word "son." *Does he know?* He looked at his father and said, "I know we've never meet, but you've always been a part of my life. My mother's name is Frances."

The man rose to his feet, took a deep breath, and with the same authoritative voice Austin had admired earlier, said, "I don't know what lies she's told you, but I'm not your father. I dated your mother in high school, but we went our separate ways when I left for college. She tried to pin that pregnancy thing on me, but I never believed her. You need to keep going down the list of all her boyfriends. I'm not your man—I'm not your father! I don't need any trouble out of you. I have a lovely family and I don't want you bothering me again. Now, if you will excuse me, I have work to do."

Stunned, Austin stood in silence. Before leaving, he turned and looked back at the man and said, "You're right, you're not my father. You don't deserve to be."

As Austin told his story, he paused to wipe a tear from his eye, and said, "I don't have a father—and I don't have a dream anymore." Heartbroken, he sat in our office, determined to salvage a faltering marriage, while fighting off demons of his past. His obsessions with perfection and control, his temper tantrums, and his overall unhappiness had nothing to do with his lovely wife and child. In order for his marriage to survive, Austin had to deal with his past before he could have any hope for the future.

When the Son Says, 'I Have a Right to Meet Him'

Sooner or later, a son that has not had contact with his father for many years will demand information on how to find him. Depending on the reason for the father's absence, the son usually will already have been given limited data to conjure an image of a phantom father that may or may not match what he has been told by his mother.

The imagined image of this phantom father will reflect the son's own hurt, anger, confusion and dreams. The imagined father may be mean and cruel, or he may border on sainthood, or he may be seen as a victim to be protected.

Unfortunately, the mother is usually the recipient of the son's displaced feelings. Since the father is unavailable to the son, he tends to shower his mother with a barrage of emotions, often vacillating from rage, hurt and anger, to depression and withdrawal.

When the son assumes a protective stance, it is usually not done to protect the father, but rather to protect the son himself. Feeling betrayed and unworthy of love, the son assumes that all negative comments about his father are untrue, the result of a conspiracy. He assumes that his mother distorts information to make herself look good and to try to foster ill will towards the father.

We advise mothers to give their sons factual information about their fathers, if requested. A mother may feel that she is sheltering her son from more hurt by withholding the truth, but as the son matures into adolescence and starts to question his mother, we recommend that she share information in an honest, straight-forward manner.

This can be an extremely difficult, especially if the mother is still hurting from pain, real or imagined, caused by the father, but it is important that she stay focused on separating the two relationships and allow the son the opportunity to find the father.

Without truthful information, the son may blame the mother for his father's absence and he may suspect that there are underlying issues that he doesn't know about.

Facing the reality that his biological father does not want to acknowledge him, or accept him as his son, is a very difficult concept for a son to accept. Good outcomes for resolving this type of rejection usually do not happen without professional counseling.

Advice for Mothers When the Father is Absent

- Share negative facts about the father only after the son is mature enough to understand that he cannot take responsibility for or change his father's behavior.
- Be honest. Admit that both you and his father made bad choices.
- In single adoptions, or arranged single pregnancies, acknowledge that you understand your son's feelings that he wants both a mother and a father.
- Seek counseling for your son when he feels that he is ready to find and confront his father. This process is always an emotional roller coaster, even when the reunion is positive.
- Never try to undermine the relationship between the father and your son, for that can only lead to bad things. You must remember at all times that your son loves the man you may want to forget. Nothing you can ever do will change that. You should not feel like you are in competition.
- If the father is in prison, a mother needs to encourage a relationship with the father if the father is willing to admit responsibility for his behavior. Try to keep your own hurt and anger out of the decision. No matter what conflicts exist between you and your son's father, they have a right to have a relationship and you should support it.
- In the event of the father's involvement in criminal or abusive behavior, we recommend that the mother seek counsel with both an attorney and a therapist. Fostering a relationship may or may not be in your son's best interest. This should be discussed with professionals on an individual case basis.
- Seek counseling when re-marriage is a possibility. Do not hope things will go well simply because you want everyone to be happy. A stepfather does not replace a father. The older the child, the more difficult the transition.
- Remember that "blended families" are very complicated and stressful for everyone involved. Seek counseling at the first sign of trouble.

Heterosexual Couples Who Adopt

We have been involved in literally hundreds of heterosexual-couple adoptions, whether counseling parents and children, or actually placing children in foster and adoptive homes. We would hate to think of a world in which adoption was not an option for children who have been abandoned for one reason or another. Adoptive moms and dads are some of the most motivated parents in our society. They put great thought and planning into building their families. The children that they envision in their lives are not a byproduct of passion or miscalculation: They are an integral part of how they see themselves as adults.

Having said that we must point out that the dynamics of the Unfriendly World Syndrome are the same for adoptive parents as they are for natural parents. The good news is that if a couple adopts a boy in infancy they have good odds of beating the ill effects of the syndrome. However, the older the child is at the time of adoption, the more difficult it is to achieve harmony.

Most boys that were adopted post-infancy are going to undergo the same emotions that sons without fathers experience as they advance in age. That is not what adoptive fathers want to hear, we know that—but the more information that adoptive parents have, the better the odds of success. The advice that we give to adoptive mothers is the same that we give to mothers of sons without fathers.

Can Two Mothers = One Father?

Sometimes mothers try to bypass the male role-model issue by having their mothers move into the household with them, thinking that two female role models will somehow compensate for the lack of a male role model.

There is evidence that two-mother family structures do no harm for young children and may contribute to the well-being of the family by providing the mother more time to play with her children. However, studies have shown that teenagers raised in mother/grandmother homes fare worse than those raised by mothers alone. Sociologists Sara McLanahan and Gary Sandefur report that children raised in mother-grandmother homes produce children that are twice as likely to drop out of school. Clearly, two mothers do not equal one father, where teenage boys are concerned.

Mother-grandmother pairings probably do no harm with younger children because they consider the grandmother to be the "daddy." Grandmother, because she is older and more experienced, invariably offers advice to the mother in the presence of the child regarding what clothes should be worn, what food should be eaten, etc. That makes sense to a six-year-old, since the grandmother looks older and is usually physically larger than the mother, but teens see through that facade. They understand that the grandmother is not a substitute for their father and it disturbs them at a primal level to see their mother bossed around by her mother. After all, that is one of the great fears expressed by teens—the possibility that their mother will always be telling them what to do—often expressed by the phrase, "Oh, Mother, just leave me alone!"

Teenage sons are also affected by what they see when they are in public with their mother and grandmother. They both may be the boss at home, but if the son sees males open doors for them, or otherwise extend courtesies to them, he interprets those gestures as acknowledgments that his mother and grandmother are submissive to males. We've seen heterosexual mothers and grandmothers make a deliberate effort to be more masculine to fulfill a fatherly role, but that never works with bright teens who invariably see through the ruse and end up suffering embarrassment among their friends.

No matter how hard they try, mothers and grandmothers cannot become fathers in the eyes of the son. The harder they try to fill that role, the more damage they do. However, there are many positive things they can do. They can respect the distance their son and grandson need from them in areas such as sports. They can encourage his interests in any activities in which he can express his identity as a male. And they can make an effort to find him suitable male role models to help guide him through the trauma of adolescence.

We have no problem with mother-grandmother families. They have a great deal to offer, as long as the mother and grandmother do not offer confusing role models to the boys in the family, especially teens who are confused about their own place in society. Teenage boys have to deal with surging hormones that often make them question their own sanity. The last thing they need to worry about is their mother's sanity. Just keep it consistently loving in the home—and, above all else, *simple!*

Lesbian Couples
The Rules Are the Same

Adoption creates a dilemma for lesbian couples. If they adopt a female child, society will cast a suspicious eye toward them, fearful that they may have a dark and possibly abusive intent for wanting to share their life with a child. That's not fair, of course, but it is social prejudice that they must confront to be effective parents.

On the other hand, if they adopt a male child, society's fears are assuaged, but new problems arise in the parenting arena. As far as the Unfriendly World Syndrome is concerned, boys raised by lesbians are in the same situation as boys parented by single moms who live with their mothers. Two mothers do not equal one father, regardless of the gender roles played by the women in their relationship with each other.

There is no reason why a lesbian couple cannot raise a happy son as long as they accept the fact that he has a need for a male role model. Our advice for lesbian couples is to follow the same guidelines we suggest for mothers of sons without fathers. Everything in this book that applies to single mothers also applies to lesbian mothers.

CHAPTER 6

Boys Trying to Cope
Through Self Treatment

Louis Armstrong is one of the most beloved musicians in American history. But his fame was a poor substitute for what he needed most growing up—a father. Born on August 4, 1901, in a New Orleans ghetto that was famously unfriendly, even to sons with fathers, Armstrong was abandoned by his father on the day he was born.

"The next time we heard of him, he had gone into an uptown neighborhood and made several other children by another woman," Armstrong wrote in Louis Armstrong: In His Own Words. "Whether he married the other woman, we're not sure. One thing—he did not marry [my mother]. She had to struggle all by herself, bringing us up. Mama Lucy [Louis's sister] and I were bastards from the start."

There is no indication that Louis's mother, or his grandmother, who actually cared for him for the first seven years of his life, ever tried to find him a male role model, but he found an unlikely one himself, sort of by accident. From the age of seven to twelve, Armstrong worked for a Russian Jew, a ragman named Morris Karnofsky. The ragman paid him to help collect bottles and rags, and to accompany him when he made coal deliveries. One day Armstrong spotted a battered cornet in a pawnshop. He dearly wanted to own it, but the five-dollar price tag was out of his reach.

Seeing how much Armstrong wanted the instrument, Karnofsky loaned him two dollars so that he could purchase the horn on the "lay-a-way" plan, whereby he paid two dollars down and fifty cents a week until it was paid in full. When he finally was able to take the horn home,

Karnofsky and his wife helped him clean and polish it and then encouraged him to learn to play it.

Karnofsky was the first father figure Armstrong ever knew.

When the Karnofskys moved to the white section of town, where Morris went into another line of work, Armstrong was left without a job—or a mentor. Not surprisingly, he dropped out of school and left his mother's house to live on the street with other homeless children.

As an adult, Armstrong was a classic Unfriendly World son. He was unable to relate to women in any way other than physically, and even that was based solely on his sexual needs. He was resentful of male authority figures, but he was too inept at dealing with other men to be confrontational; instead, he simply went with the flow, doing what he was told, masking his frustration with alcohol and marijuana.

Armstrong married poorly the first time, choosing a prostitute with whom he often fought. He met his second wife, Lil Hardin, when he left New Orleans and moved to Chicago to play in King Oliver's Creole Jazz Band, which featured Lil on piano. She couldn't stand him at first—she particularly disliked the "country" way he dressed—but she soon fell in love with him and they were married after they divorced their spouses.

Lil was a perfect match for Armstrong. She taught him how to dress and how to behave around other men—something he might have learned if he had had a father in the home—and she helped him organize a band of his own and she wrote songs for the band to record. Of course, their marriage was doomed from the beginning. Armstrong was unable to maintain a long-term relationship with her or any other women.

He was unfaithful to her, almost from the beginning.

Armstrong went on to enjoy a fabulous career, while going through another marriage or two, but throughout his life he was unable to maintain close friendships with other males—not even his own bandmates—preferring instead the company of women.

Laurence Bergreen, an Armstrong biographer, put it well when he wrote: "His father had given him nothing, not a word of advice, no legacy, no acknowledgment that he even was his father, only a lingering sense of failure, frustration, and anger. For that, the boy felt he owed the old man nothing in return."

Armstrong couldn't say enough good things about his mother—"My mother and grandmother were the people who raised me, specially [sic] my mother. She said, 'Son, you got a chance. Don't waste it.'"—but he never got over not having a father and he was angry about that until the day he died.

The music world can be grateful that his mother and grandmother stepped into the void and did the best they could under the circumstances. They kept the youngster together body and soul. But, as important as those contributions were it seems obvious that Armstrong's ultimate survival depended more on a fortuitous encounter with the only male role model he ever had in childhood—the Jewish ragman.

Positive Outcomes through Self-Treatment

Louis Armstrong was rejected by his father at conception. Knowing you were never wanted is a lingering pain that can never be soothed. Armstrong and many other sons never form a father-son bond to be later broken. The hard lessons of life were learned early and Armstrong never seemed to spend much time lamenting that life is not fair. Through adversity he seemed to gain strength.

Armstrong forged ahead into what he felt was an unfriendly world. With the encouragement of his Jewish ragman mentor, Armstrong found a painkiller that worked for him . . . music. His five-dollar cornet gave him hope, an ambition and eventually an escape from the poverty of the New Orleans slums. One can only guess at how his life would have been affected if his father had claimed him, loved him and encouraged him.

Self-treatment can take on many faces. Armstrong turned to the arts for his therapeutic remedy for life's pain. Others turn to academic achievement, sports, or writing, with positive outcomes. Sons without fathers have to re-focus, re-group and approach the world differently than those who sit and discuss life goals, make plans and lean on their father for support. The fatherless son feels alone, no matter how much his mother may be there for him. It's simply not the same. Embracing the reality of life, a son without a father must face his Unfriendly World. He can either use his strength to conquer—or withdraw and declare defeat.

Unfriendly World sons who choose positive self-treatment are often among our greatest achievers. They often become famous leaders, researchers, writers, artists, actors and politicians. They achieve by channeling their pain in a productive direction. Not surprisingly, the above-mentioned areas of achievement all have one thing in common: They all require varying amounts of something that most people fear—isolation.

Families sometimes become concerned when the son finds relief in isolation since it is a symptom of many potentially disturbing conditions. Isolation can have very positive—or very negative—effects, depending on the child. If he spends time drawing, writing, studying or engaging in other productive activity, isolation can be therapeutic. However, parents should be cautious about a son who is unwilling to let his parents know what he's doing during his time alone. Alcohols, drugs, pornography, and the planning of violent or criminal acts are usually done in secret.

Isolation for the purpose of focus can be beneficial. Unfriendly World sons may not want to be the life of the party. They are distrustful of people who enjoy life too much. They are often more comfortable alone in their own bedroom. Why should he interact with the world that mistreated him? Armstrong expressed his pain through his music. He avoided his hurt while he played music and he achieved self-value and respect by his accomplishments. His cornet became his friend, his companion and the mechanism by which he proved himself. The words, rhythm, and style of his music became his voice of suffering and pain.

Tom Cruise also self-treated himself in a positive way. His academic problems were overshadowed by successes on the stage. Acting helped him prove to himself that he was worthy of respect. In recent years, acting has allowed him to demonstrate his physical abilities. He is more daring than most, a risk taker, and a perfectionist. Through adversity, he has become a very supportive father to his two children.

Joltin' Joe DiMaggio:
No Home Runs for Namesake

Baseball legend Joe DiMaggio was as authentic a hero as one can find in American sports. The winner of three "Most Valuable Player" awards, he was one of the most heralded players to ever wear a New York Yankees uniform. With a career batting average of .325—and 361 home runs to his credit—he was elected to the Baseball Hall of Fame in 1955. Many people consider him the best baseball player who ever lived.

The son of Sicilian immigrants, Joe DiMaggio grew up in San Francisco with four brothers and four sisters. His father, Giuseppe, was strictly a man of old-world sensibilities. He was strict with his children, but preferred that his wife discipline them. Despite Giuseppe's macho posturing, it was Mama who was really in charge of the family—and all the children understood that.

Even though Giuseppe's biggest dream was that his five sons would go into business with him, he was never demonstrative in his approval of their actions. As a result, with no positive feedback from their father, each of them quietly went their separate ways.

Joe's career path led to a baseball stadium. By the age of 19, he was a celebrity in the Bay City area, playing with a minor league baseball team named the San Francisco Seals. Joe was shy around girls, so it took a while for him to find the girl of his dreams and settle down.

Eventually, Joe married a Hollywood actress named Dorothy Arnold. Two years later, she gave him a son they named Joe DiMaggio, Jr. (they called him Joey). By then, Joe was playing with the New York Yankees and was the toast of baseball. Joey's birth was treated as a news event. Joe was photographed holding his son at every opportunity.

Unfortunately, when he wasn't holding his son for photographers, he quickly tossed him to Dorothy and left the house to pal around with his friends and admirers. He didn't seem to realize it, but he was raising Joey exactly as he had been raised—with as little personal contact as possible.

When Dorothy filed for divorce after three years of marriage, no one was surprised, except Joe, who had a hard time believing that she would divorce him. According to biographer Richard Ben Cramer, Joe "never knew how much he wanted to keep her until she'd walked away. He never gave up on what was his."

Joe and Dorothy tried reconciliation, but that didn't work because their hearts and minds were in different places. She remarried and raised Joey with the help of a nanny, but Joe lost interest in his son by the time the child was eight, perhaps because he reminded him too much of Dorothy and of how she had rejected him. Around the time that Joe bowed out of being a father to Joey, Dorothy decided to send her son off to a boarding school, thus separating him from both mother and father.

As he grew into manhood, Joey tried to please his father, but nothing seemed to work. Joey was symbolic of one of his father's greatest failures—and if there was one thing Joe couldn't tolerate, it was failure. Joey didn't understand that, of course. All he knew was that his famous father wasn't interested in spending time with him.

Joey could have been a poster child for the Unfriendly World Syndrome. He had a mother who loved him but didn't know how to raise him without a father. And he had a father who, despite his unquestioned status as an American hero, simply couldn't find a way to connect with his son.

Father and son seldom saw each other, but even that sporadic contact ended in the late 1960s, when Joey wandered onto a houseboat in Miami where Larry King was broadcasting a radio program. With a little encouragement from King, Joey got behind the microphone and spoke, for the first time publicly about his childhood.

"I never knew my father," he told the radio audience, according to King. "My . . . father was totally missing from my childhood. When they needed a picture of father and son, I'd get picked up in a limo and have my picture taken . . . I was driven to the photo session, we had the picture taken, and I was driven back. My father and I didn't say two words."

107

Joe was outraged by what he considered a betrayal. What right did his son have to talk about his life in such intimate terms? After the interview, their relationship went from cool to icy cold. Joe set his son up in a business that made polyurethane foam, but it folded after some disagreements with the other partners. Then he bought a $75,000 truck for Joey, a vehicle that he could use to support himself making long-haul deliveries.

There was one last point at which Joey and his father could have reconciled, according to biographer Cramer. When he was in his late twenties, Joey married a young woman named Sue who had two toddler daughters. Eager for his father to meet her, he took her to Scottsdale, Arizona, where Joe was participating in a golf tournament. That evening, Joey and Sue joined Joe and a couple of his friends for dinner in the resort's main dining room. Joey had already made one mistake. That morning he had come down the stairs to the lobby wearing blue jeans. Joe promptly ordered him to return to his room and dress properly. Sue made the second big mistake at dinner, when she tapped her fingers against the table in time with the music.

"Step outside," Joe told his son. "I want to talk to you."

With Joe, it was two strikes and you're out!

After their conversation, Joey returned to the table and told Sue they had to leave right away and return to San Francisco. After they left the table, a female friend of Joe's ran after them and asked for an explanation for their sudden departure. Replied Joey: "My father said he doesn't want anything to do with her."

Soon Joey was abusing alcohol and drugs on a grand scale. He wrecked the truck and then lost his trucker's license. He got a job driving a cement truck in Las Vegas, but he made it clear to everyone that if his father called they were to say they did not know where he was. Father and son remained estranged, up until Joe's death in 1999.

Joey went to his father's funeral wearing a new suit, with his long, gray hair pulled back into a ponytail out of respect for his father. Later Joey learned that his father had only left him an annual stipend of

$20,000. Considering his vast wealth, it was a disappointingly small amount and in Joey's eyes a final rejection of him as his son.

Six months after the funeral, Joey died from an overdose of heroin mixed with crack cocaine.

Negative Outcomes Through Self-Treatment

What better life could a young boy dream of than to be born to a true American sports hero? Sadly, young Joey was a news event, not a personal pleasure for his father. Joe DiMaggio may have been the "best baseball player" that ever lived, but he won no "best father" awards for his parenting. After years of self-treatment with a combination of illegal drugs, Joey struck out one last time. He felt beaten down by his famous father's rejection. He was angry with himself, his father, and the Unfriendly World he lived in.

As often happens, Joe DiMaggio turned into his own father—a man who failed to love, nurture and support his children. The attention and fame he enjoyed probably served to heal some of his emotional wounds. As his own success grew, he developed feelings of self-worth, something his own father failed to encourage; but amide the glory and praise, stood a lonely son of an immigrant, who would only repeat history by rejecting his own son. Unfortunately, the outcome of the latter rejection may have resulted in the ultimate negative self-treatment, a drug overdose.

Joey lived up to his own self-image of a failure. He never measured up to his father's expectations, and never won his love or respect. With his death, he screamed one last plea for his father to care about him. It was like screaming into the wind.

Although it is too late for Joe DiMaggio and his son, Joey, to learn from their mistakes, it is not too late for us to learn from them. Parents must watch for risk factors of substance use as early as elementary school. Sons without fathers are at higher risk for the type of experimentation that often leads to drug abuse.

Mothers sometimes can be naïve about the severity of their son's problems. The loss of a girlfriend, failing a test, not making the team, loosing a school election—all may seem fairly insignificant to mothers. They should take notice if their son cannot solve his problems and then move on. If a mother sees her son obsessing about problems that seem simple to the parent, they should seek counseling for the child. Mothers should not minimize their children's problems.

Do not be reluctant to discuss your concerns openly with your son. Talking about drug abuse with your son does not push him towards it.

The National Institute on Drug Abuse and Alcoholism estimates that there are over three million teenage alcoholics in America. The average age when children first try alcohol is eleven years for boys and thirteen for girls. Adolescents who begin drinking before age fifteen are four times more likely to develop alcohol dependence than young adults who begin drinking at age twenty-one.

Fatherless homes dramatically affect the behavior of adolescents when it comes to drugs and alcohol. One study reports that a father's presence is five times more important than all other factors considered in adolescent alcohol and marijuana use.

When alcohol or other substances cloud the judgment of sons without fathers, the combination can have deadly results. Fatherless sons may use drugs and alcohol to help compensate for the loss of a father, and to obtain a sense of power in their ever-seeking quest to conquer the unfriendly world around them.

Quentin Tarantino
Pass the Violence, Please

Some people look at Quentin Tarantino and see a masterful film-maker, the creative force behind films such as Reservoir Dogs and Pulp Fiction. We look at Quentin Tarantino and see an Unfriendly World child who has used violent imagery to self-treat his pain of growing up without a father.

Born in Knoxville, Tennessee, to a sixteen-year-old mother, Tarantino, now in his late forties, never knew his father because he disappeared before he was born. His mother, who later earned a nursing degree, took her son to Los Angeles, where she thought she would find more job opportunities as a single mother.

Once in Los Angeles, she moved often and subjected her son to a series of substitute fathers, one of whom she married, according to a profile in Vanity Fair: "He skipped school at every opportunity, hiding in the bathroom until his mother went to work, spending the rest of the day at home, burying himself in comics books and television—every mother's nightmare."

Tarantino once told an interviewer that one of his father figures during that time was a black man who rented a room in their home. He described the man as a con-man who allowed him—he was fifteen at the time—to wear his pimp-style clothing as a way of standing out among his adolescent peers.

Tarantino identified with African Americans, probably because most of the black males he came into contact with were sons without fathers. Not surprisingly, he told Adrian Wootton of The Guardian that "some of the people in my life I have admired the most were older black women. I have a lot of respect for them."

Writer Elmore Leonard once made the mistake of asking Tarantino why he was so fond of the 1958 classic film, Rio Bravo, a story about a stand-up-guy sheriff, played by John Wayne, who organizes a group of losers to right a wrong.

"He just went on and on, opening with, 'You know . . . . I didn't have a father.'

"Uh-oh," Leonard thought.

Growing up, Tarantino obviously felt a great deal of pain over not having a father. He tried to self-treat that pain with a rich fantasy life that symbolically expressed his suppressed rage in more socially accepted ways than if he had acted them out on the street, which is what happens all too often.

One only has to view the film-maker's movies to understand how those childhood pains have affected him as an adult. Tarantino is a classic product of an Unfriendly World childhood. Everywhere he looks, he sees violence and implied threats—and that viewpoint is reflected in his work. But once you get past the violence (and more often than not, the violence is implied, not actual), you see that there is a core of redemption and forgiveness in his work. He wants to believe that goodness is possible in everyone.

Rip the angry mask away from an adult son-without-a-father and, invariably, you will find a dreamer who desperately wants to believe that goodness is possible, if only the bad people of the earth, especially those with real-life fathers, could be relocated to a faraway galaxy.

Picking Up the Pieces

Sons without fathers agree with Mr. Roger's concept of the world being "not a kind place," which may be one reason why so many children during that era of friendly television watched his program as they were growing up. Mr. Rogers provided an alternate view of the universe. In real life, they often witness the conflicts between their parents before a divorce and then they become part of the conflict afterwards. A son may overhear his mother on the phone with the father pleading for more child support money. He may see the frustration in his mother's eyes when she can't juggle all the demands of single parenting and still have the energy and time to laugh and play with the family.

He feels the hurt, pain and anger of the world. He expects bad things to happen every time he steps out the door. He's overly cautious and willing to take on anyone who crosses his path. He isolates himself to cope with his unhappiness and self-doubts. His tendency to strike out at the world around him may be expressed in a variety of ways.

Tarantino used the silver screen to express his anger. Of course, he saw plenty of violence in his neighborhood, but he somehow managed to survive that and channel his energy in a way that gave him an acceptable outlet. He became famous in the process. That is a common trait of sons

112

without fathers: They don't give up. They are tenacious and willing to fight for their cause. They fully believe that the world will not overlook anything. There are no breaks out there waiting for them—and they are convinced that they must create their own opportunities.

Tarantino's mother made some unwise decisions along the way, but her willingness to allow her son to pursue his creative energies was exactly the right thing to do. Without that outlet, he would have been unable to self-treat his emotional wounds and would, most likely, have ended up a grim statistic.

Mothers don't have to be perfect to raise healthy sons, but if they don't have the right instincts—as Tarantino's mother demonstrated—then they need all the good information they can gather, which is why we wrote this book.

Of this we are certain: Every mother's son can be the exception.

CHAPTER 7

Nurturing Self-Control and Empathy

The furious mother stormed into the office, tossed her purse onto a nearby table, and then sat down hard in the chair across from the desk, rolling her eyes skyward.

"My ex-husband drives me crazy," she said, sighing after every other word. "All he does is play silly games with Johnny. I am the one who takes him to the doctor and to school—and he gets to be the hero and have all the fun. He should be doing something important with his son. You know, teaching him something!"

What the mother didn't understand was that her son's father already was filling a very important role in their son's development. It is through games that boys learn enough self-control to respond in a positive manner to parental discipline.

Dad's "silly" games all have rules:

"Three strikes and you're out!"

"If you cross this line, you're out of bounds!"

"You are down when your knee touches the ground!"

"You have too many men on the field!"

"You threw it too high to be a strike!"

"You dropped the ball!"

"The ball landed past the line!"

"That's an illegal tackle—you've got to pay a penalty!"

And so it goes.

Boys learn cause and effect from their dads. They learn that when they break the rules, they must be penalized—and that means they are at greater risk to *lose*! When they play a game with dad—and dad wins—that means they lose. Little boys like to win. Moms have a more difficult time disciplining boys because they are not the parent who taught them about winning and losing.

Athletics are important for boys, not so much for the physical exercise (though with children today becoming increasingly obese, the importance of exercise increases), or because of the teamwork it requires (or the competitiveness it engenders), but because of the gamesmanship involved. Non-athletic games, such as card or board games (or even computer games) accomplish the same function as sports.

What may appear frivolous to the mother is one of the most important building blocks in her son's development. When we describe a child as a "problem child," one who will not obey adults, what we are really saying is that he does not exhibit good self-control. No child wants to be punished for misbehavior. There is nothing about punishment that a child enjoys. He indulges in forbidden behavior because he does not have the self-control necessary to put on the brakes. Boys who are good at playing games with other people are usually good at accepting discipline.

Men and women sometimes have opposing approaches to discipline. Mothers soon learn that the best way to avoid the need for discipline is to allow their son to watch television for hours at a time. The biggest problem with that, aside from subjecting them to dubious programming, is the fact that children who spend all their time watching television do not learn the play skills they need.

It never ceases to amaze us when we hear mothers complain that their sons, who have just spent four hours watching television, are suddenly difficult to discipline once they tire of that activity. Watching television is not a substitute for play activity; it teaches children nothing about self-control or negotiating with their playmates for what they want. If watching television is a good activity, why do parents invariably end up sending their children to their rooms for punishment for some misdeed once the television programming has ended?

Single mothers sometimes use television as a defense against discipline. When that doesn't work they *threaten* to take away privileges or they *threaten* to tell daddy when he picks up the son. They spank them as a last resort, primarily because it upsets them to strike their children.

Fathers are just the opposite. They urge the child to "go outside and play," instead of watching television. Admittedly, there may be a selfish motivation involved, especially if there is a sports event that dad wants to watch on television.

Fathers seldom threaten to punish; they usually do it on the spot. That is what boys expect because that is what they have been taught while playing games with their dad. It's not three strikes you're out *later*. Its three strikes you're out *right now*. Fathers spank their sons as a means of demonstrating physical dominance, something that becomes increasingly importance as boys head into adolescence.

We refer to spanking here only to explain what happens in typical families. We don't recommend striking children at any age for any reason. Whatever advantages we are tempted to see in mothers and fathers paddling children for bad behavior are erased by our experience with parents who physically abuse their children. We've seen mothers who spanked infants (only to have them placed in a foster home) and fathers who have beaten sons or daughters so severely that the children had to be hospitalized.

The reason so many parents spank their children is because it is often an effective short-term remedy to bad behavior. The problem with that, even when done lightly, is that the parent is also teaching lessons while administering punishment. They are teaching that violence is all right in some situations. They are teaching that one acceptable result of anger is violence. And they are associating violence with authority.

We will never forget the two boys, aged six and seven, who were given a sound spanking by their parents and abandoned on a city street corner. When we arrived at the police station the boys were sitting on a wooden bench in the waiting area. There was a small wire cage on the bench between them. In the cage was a white dove.

The sight of the brothers, paralyzed by fright and wide-eyed with uncertainty, while desperately clinging to their only possession, a solitary morning dove, was heart-breaking, not just because of what had happen to them, but because of what we knew lay ahead for them. We placed them in a loving foster home, where the foster mother instinctively won them over by making a big fuss over their feathered traveling companion.

Within days their parents were tracked down by the police and arrested. When they were interviewed, they said they had abandoned their two sons because they "did not mind." The father, who seemed surprised that abandoning children was against the law, explained that the more they spanked the boys, the worse their behavior became. "Finally, it just got to the point where they were bringing us down," he explained. "It was either them or us—you know."

If you are spanking your child, you should stop, take a deep breath, and look for the source of the problem. If your child is misbehaving— and the disciplinary actions you administer are growing in frequency— increase the child's playtime with dad (or a male role model substitute). The worst thing you can do as a parent is to deprive your child of playtime with dad as a punishment. Children aren't born bad seeds. They become what you allow them to become.

Recognize spankings for what they are: A failure of parenting. Also, consider that if your spankings are successful, they are successful only for specific behavior. What you are saying with a spanking is, "Don't do that again or I'll wear you out!" The child associates the spanking only with the behavior in question. For that reason, spankings fail to teach children self-control. How can spanking teach self-control, especially if a parent spanks when she is angry? Self-control in children occurs when parents are successful in instilling a playtime mentality in them children—break the rules and you loose! It is a lesson that applies to both parent and child. Try calmly saying, "I'm sorry you chose to misbehave. The consequence of your behavior is _____!"

Understanding Empathy

Empathy is the most important survival skill a boy can possess. Some people consider empathy to be a "sissy" characteristic, one that makes boys too softhearted. Nothing could be further from the truth.

Secret Service agents, those who out their lives on the line to protect the president, possess high degrees of empathy. They must evaluate minute changes in behavior in an instant. Empathy is a survival skill that allows boys to not only care about what others are feeling, but to make accurate judgments in a wide range of social situations. Without empathy, boys would be unable to determine if people are uneasy, despondent, horrified, bored, cautious, playful, irritated, relieved, shy, hostile, dangerous, annoyed or preoccupied. A boy without empathy is a disaster waiting to happen. Of all the skills fathers teach their sons, it is empathy that is the most important.

* * *

When three-time world heavyweight boxing champion Muhammad Ali (his birth name was Cassius Marcellus Clay Jr.) was born in 1942 in Louisville, Kentucky, America was still a good two decades away from accepting the fact that African Americans had the same rights as light-skinned citizens. Racial segregation infected every segment of society, including the family unit, which was structured by white society in such a way as to minimize the contributions of male African Americans.

In the 1940s and 1950s, when Ali was coming of age, African-American families were expected to be matriarchal, with fathers relegated to a secondary status. Not surprisingly, fathers tended to move from family to family, conceiving new children as they went, thus giving African-American families the largest percentage of Unfriendly World children of the various racial and ethnic groups.

Ali's family was different. His mother, Odessa Clay, was the undisputed boss of the family insofar as the children were concerned, but his father, Cassius Clay Sr., took his parental responsibilities seriously and never abandoned his family. As a result, Ali beat the odds and grew up with his father in the home.

Cassius Sr. was not a perfect father by any means—he had an arrest record for disorderly conduct and reckless driving, and his wife had to call police for protection on three different occasions—but he did spend time with his children.

"I made sure they were around good people; not people who would bring them into trouble," he told biographer Thomas Hauser. "And I taught them values—always confront the things you fear, try to be the best at whatever you do. That's what my daddy taught me, and those are things that have to be taught. You don't learn those things by accident."

A sign painter by trade, Cassius Sr. sometimes took Ali with him when he went out on a job. He taught him how to draw letters and mix the paint, and he taught him how to interact with other men. As a result, from the age of twelve, Ali felt comfortable seeking out males who could teach him other things, such as boxing.

Ali's first male mentor was a white highway patrolman named Joe Martin, who hosted a television show called "Tomorrow's Champions." He arranged for Ali to work out at a local gym, where a black trainer named Fred Stoner taught him the mechanics of boxing. There is more to boxing than throwing and ducking punches, of course, and Stoner taught Ali how to read the faces of his opponents. It takes a great deal of empathy to be a championship boxer. To be successful you must be able to determine their intentions and then act to counteract them with lightning speed.

As a result of all that positive male attention and instruction, Ali was able to grow into what many would consider a "man's man," all the while developing an uncommonly strong set of ethical and religious beliefs. Ali attributed those beliefs to his mother.

"Every Sunday, she dressed me up, took me and my brother to church, and taught us the way she thought was right," Ali told Hauser. "She taught us to love people and treat everybody with kindness. She taught us it was wrong to be prejudiced or hate . . .there's no one who's been better to me my whole life."

Ali displayed empathy toward others throughout his career, beginning with his refusal in 1966 to be drafted to fight in Vietnam (at the time, newspapers were filled with reports of violence against women and children in the war zone), by his involvement in the emerging civil rights movement—among African Americans, only Martin Luther King had a higher profile—and by the way he worked to promote world peace.

In 2000, the United Nations named Ali a Messenger of Peace, with a citation that read: ". . . through your contributions to sports and human rights, the message of peace, harmony and human dignity will resound throughout the nations."

As a child, Ali had everything in the world going against him—he was the wrong color for success in America, his family barely had enough money to get by, and he performed poorly in school. What he had going for him was a kind and compassionate mother, a father who never abandoned him despite several close calls, and male mentors who believed in him and taught him survival skills. Ali is the best example we know of how empathy works as a survival skill.

Empathy as a Window on the World

Mom feels that she is being a bad mother if she ever frowns at her child, or shows displeasure. She wants her child to know only a friendly universe. Dad feels that he is being a bad father if he does not make it clear from the beginning that the world has quite a bite to it if certain rules are not followed.

Whether those attitudes are biological or cultural is really beside the point. Parents must raise children to live in the real world, not some vision of how the world should be, so as long as our culture supports and advocates gender differences in parenting, responsible parents have no choice but to address those differences.

Women seem to have a natural ability to empathize with others. The word "empathy" is generally understood to mean having sympathy for another person's situation. That's part of the empathy process, but it is more complicated than that. Empathy also means the ability to evaluate a person's feelings by their body language and facial expressions.

Biblical definitions aside, what we call morality is actually the ability to make decisions based on a judgment of whether our actions will help or hurt other people. Often our only clue is based on a reading of body language and facial expressions. If a child does not have that ability, he will have a difficult time judging the appropriateness of his actions. One definition of a psychopath is someone who is without empathy for others. The masked gunman who robs a convenience store, puts his pistol in the face of the clerk, and then pulls the trigger, has no concept of what his victim is feeling. His emotions are focused entirely on himself.

A mother can possess tons of empathy. She can be the most loving, compassionate person in the world. But nature has wired her son so that she cannot transfer significant amounts of that empathy to him. Again, there are exceptions: We can cite examples of empathetic mothers that raised empathetic sons without a father's involvement, but they are in the minority.

Centuries of evolving human development have determined that empathy is the responsibility of the father. If he fails to live up to that responsibility, the son suffers the consequences. He becomes aggressive, impulsive and prone to risky behavior.

In a report on violence, the National Research Council named several factors that their researchers found that correlated with aggressive behavior in children: "harsh and erratic discipline, lack of parental nurturance, physical abuse and neglect, poor supervision, and early separation of children from parents." It is that latter factor that we feel is the most important because it directly affects the other factors such as discipline and nurturance.

Rutgers University professor David Popenoe says that it is not clear why fathers are so important to building empathy. "Perhaps merely being with their children provides a model for compassion," he wrote in *Life Without Father*. "Perhaps it has to do with their style of play or mode of reasoning. Perhaps it is somehow related to the fact that fathers typically are the family's main arbiter with the outside world. Or perhaps it is because when mothers receive help from fathers and are thus freed from some of the instrumental demands of child-rearing, they are more able themselves to promote empathic concerns. Whatever the reason, it is hard to think of a more important contribution that fathers can make to their children."

How Much Empathy Does Your Child Have?

Your son's empathy development should progress at a steady rate from early childhood, through school age and into adolescence. Not sure where your son stands? Try this unscientific test to measure his development:

Pre-school age: Clip photos from a magazine that you think demonstrate happiness, anger and sadness—or make them yourself—then ask your son to tell you what the people in the photos are feeling. He should recognize all three expressions. If he does not, you have work to do. If he is unable to recognize anger, why are you punishing him for not recognizing anger in your face? Keep flashing the photos and asking him to identify the emotions until he is able to name the emotions depicted in the photographs.

School-age: Clip four photos that show more complicated emotional reflections of annoyance, friendliness (this emotion will differ from happiness in that eye contact is a requirement for friendliness) and surprise. If he can correctly identify all three, you are on track; if not, spend time on the areas in which he is deficient. For example, if he misses "annoyance," explain to him that it is a level below anger.

Adolescent: Ask your son a series of questions that address emotions that you want him to be able to identify. For example, ask him if he can tell the difference between when you are angry at him or simply frustrated over outside events that do not even involve him. Use specific examples of past situations if it will help get him started. He should be able to describe the differences between those two emotions.

Another question could be to ask him if he knows the difference between when you are preoccupied or expressing disapproval over his actions. He should be able to discern that you are preoccupied if you say, "Can we talk about this later," or if you respond to his questions with a series of, "uh-huh, uh-huh." If you are expressing disapproval of something he has done, he should be able to recognize that by your critical comments. Do not postpone correcting your son when he has done something wrong. Do not say "We will talk about this later." Make time now to discuss his behavior, even if it means terminating a cell phone conversation with your best friend.

If you go through a series of questions like this, you may discover that your conversation will open the door to better overall communication. You want to encourage him to ask questions if he thinks he is misreading your feelings. In the process, you may learn that you have been misreading his feelings.

If you can't tell how much empathy your son possesses by observing him and talking to him, we have pleasurable test that you can administer to him: Give him a dog or a cat (if you don't want a pet in the household, take him to the house of a friend that has a pet). Simply hand the animal to him and watch his reaction.

Does he hold it lovingly, or does he hold it too tightly?

If he holds it too tightly—and it protests with a cry for help—does he immediately release it and comfort it—or does he maintain his tight grip?

Boys of normal development are naturally very nurturing toward pets. They hold them like babies, they cuddle them and talk "baby talk" to them, and they proudly show them off to anyone who will pay attention. Boys that are lacking in empathy are less likely to hold pets and more likely to chase them or throw things at them. They are also more likely to ridicule them and call them names such as "stupid" and "ugly."

'Wait Until I Tell Your Dad'

No divorced mom should ever say those words to a child. Unfortunately, some resort to it on a regular basis. They don't do it out of stupidity, but because they see the mere threat of dad's discipline as an effective child management tool—and because after centuries of evolution society has declared discipline to be a male domain. Even worse is when a divorced mom threatens to not let her son see his dad as punishment.

Once you take dad out of the family picture, the two issues that are most likely to send mom into a psychologist's office for help are play and discipline. The two issues are closely related. If you mix a group of preschool-age boys with fathers with an equal number without fathers—and allow them to interact without adult interference in a roomful of toys—it will soon become evident that some of the boys play better than others, and some are more aggressive in fighting for the toys they want.

Typically, the sons without fathers will overreact when they don't get the toy they want. They will shove and push and hit anyone who stands in the way. The children with fathers may or may not defend themselves, but most likely they will treat the attack as a game and grab the toy and run, resorting to the play tactics they learned from their fathers. If the son without a father is successful in seizing the toy he wants, it will soon become apparent that he doesn't know what to do with it once it is his. His attention span for play often is very short and within minutes he will discard the toy he fought for and seek a replacement.

When adults intervene in disputes over the toys, they discover that the sons without fathers find it difficult to "take no for an answer." In fact, "no" is an Unfriendly World child's favorite response when asked by an adult to change his behavior.

"No, Bob—you can't play with the ball. I want you to give it back to Billy. He was playing with it first."

"No," says the son without a father, mimicking the adult.

If at that point, Bob puts the toy behind his back when the adult reaches for it, or runs away, the adult has only one realistic option—to take the toy away, then to take Bob by the hand and lead him away from the group. The adult should have two goals: to isolate the misbehaving child for a short period and to protect the integrity of the group. Left unchallenged, sons without fathers often will instigate rebellion among the other children, even those that normally follow the rules.

If there is another adult in the room the best way to handle the situation is for one adult to take the misbehaving child outside or into another room. If you are alone with the children, you obviously cannot take the offending child out of the room since that would leave the other children unsupervised. In that situation, you should give the "good" boy a task to occupy his attention (if he is a son with a father, he will play oblivious to your presence) and take the "bad" boy to the other side of the room, where you go through the same type of play described for outside activities.

It is important for the other children to see a cause-effect relationship for misbehavior. Once the child is isolated, the adult should engage him in play. You must remember that Bob misbehaved, not because he is bad, but because no one has taught him self control.

When you reach the point that the child is smiling and laughing again, take him back inside and try to jump-start the same game with the boy that he had the confrontation with earlier. With any luck, the two boys will play well together, at least for a short time. If becomes obvious that the game is falling apart, you should separate them and direct their energies in other directions.

In general, mothers tend to terminate playtime quickly with sons after saying, "Don't!"—"Stop!"—"Not so hard!"—and other words that indicate that she is uncomfortable with the aggressiveness of his play. Moms seem to desire a quiet, peaceful activity over the rough play that their sons enjoy.

When Dads Nurture
Is it Gender Related?

Among some sociologists and psychologists there is a line of thinking that rejects gender differences between men and women. It maintains that men can do anything that women can do, and vice versa. Their philosophy, which has been labeled the "New Father model" and the "androgynous parent," can be expressed as follows:

"There is very little about the gender of a parent that is distinctly important."

"We should insist that men become more like women."

"Fathers should overcome entrenched misconceptions about fatherhood."

Our position is that if the first two statements were true, we would not currently be facing a crisis with Unfriendly World children. There is room for improvement with the idea expressed in the third statement, but there should be recognition that men and women have physical, emotional and social differences. To argue otherwise is a disservice to the children who pay the price when those differences are not addressed.

In his book *Fatherless America,* David Blankenhorn argues against the concept of creating a "New Father" standard: "The essence of the New Father model is a repudiation of gendered social roles. But fatherhood, by definition, is a gendered social role. To ungender fatherhood—to deny males any gender-based role in family life—is to deny fatherhood as a social activity. What remains may be New. But there is no more Father."

It is self-defeating to even suggest that fathers should become more androgynous. The word has both physical and psychological implications, and it is not likely to make friends for those who use it in any context.

Americans sometimes feel that they can change anything they don't like. Don't like your nose? Just get a new one. Overweight? Just get a surgeon to cut off the excess fat. Don't like your son's father? Why not just make dad into a mother?

We would like to see fathers become more nurturing, but if they relinquish their cultural role as fathers they are doing the psychological equivalent of allowing their sons to grow up without a father. For sons, at least, the better alternative to making their father androgynous would be to make their mothers more masculine. That's not going to happen, either.

Sons need a parent that nurtures—and a parent that encourages them to engage in risk-taking behavior. Nature did not wire boys to have both needs filled by the same gender.

John O'Hara
Tough Nurturing

When Patrick O'Hara was a young adult attending college, friends told his father, Mike, that he was seen drinking in a saloon. That was especially grievous news because Patrick's brother Martin had died after getting drunk and falling under the wheels of a moving train. Mangled, he was brought home to die on the sofa in the family living room.

Patrick's father told him that he didn't want the same thing to happen to him and he administered the temperance oath to him, an act that made Patrick duty bound not to drink until he was twenty-one. After that age, Patrick refrained from drinking, simply because he thought it would interfere with his main goal in life—becoming a surgeon.

Later in life, when Patrick married and had a family of his own, he maintained that same attitude toward alcohol abuse. It wasn't so much a moral issue as it was a family issue.

Then along came Patrick's son, novelist John O'Hara, who didn't see what all the fuss was about. When he was sent off to college, he rebelled against family tradition.

To a friend, according to biographer Finis Farr, he wrote that he and his father were at odds over his drinking: "This time he has good and sufficient reason to become perturbed; someone has told him of my boozing. He told me about what he had heard and made several dire threats which aren't even interesting; he hasn't the nerve to carry them out, but nevertheless, life henceforth will be a veritable hell for me. He has made it so before and he'll use every means he can to make it hell, because of all things he hates, liquor receives double its share."

Despite John's perceived injustices by his no-nonsense father, the older man, who was a revered doctor in the community, did what he could to get his son started in a profession. He very much wanted his son to follow in his footsteps as a doctor. When John was twelve, he told his son that if he would agree to pursue a career as a doctor he would deposit ten thousand dollars in a fund for his medical education.

John refused the offer. When it became apparent that medicine was not John's forte—he knew that writing was what interested him most— Patrick asked the publisher of the local newspaper to give his son a try as a reporter.

John excelled at his job, though it was not so much the news gathering that excited him, but the comradeship on the newspaper staff and the opportunity it gave him to hone his writing skills. A few years later, when John was twenty-five, his father was diagnosed with Bright's Disease, a now obsolete term for serious kidney disease.

During his final days, he was cared for by loved ones in a hospital bed that had been moved to his home. At one point, during one of his rare lucid moments, he called out to his wife, "Katharine, I'm going to die," to which she answered: "Who will take care of the children?" Patrick's answer was perhaps not what she hoped to hear: "The world will take care of them."

When the attending doctors told the family that the end was near, according to Farr, John entered his father's room and drew close to his bedside when he realized that he was trying to tell him something. As it turned out, it was his father who had the last word in their relationship.

"Poor John," he said in a faint whisper to his son, "—poor John!"

After the funeral, John wrote to a friend that his father's death had had a "sobering" effect on him. He did not mean that literally because he continued to drink heavily for another two decades, not quitting until a failed suicide attempt and a bleeding ulcer made it clear that if he wanted to continue writing he would have to stay sober. Later in life, he realized that his father had been right all along, but at what price to father and son had the lesson been learned?

Sadly, many families operate on the same principle that guided the O'Haras. There are many lessons that parents must teach their children, but all too often parents focus on one issue that—if it is ever breached, whether intentionally or by accident—results in what amounts to lifelong estrangement.

For the O'Haras, the issue was alcohol. For other families, it is politics or race or religion or choice of employment. Every day that the sun rises, a father or mother somewhere in America tells a son or daughter that if they ever cross a particular line, "you are no longer a child of mine." Sadly, too many mothers and fathers mean exactly what they say.

Patrick O'Hara was right to warn his son about the dangers associated with alcohol use, but he was wrong to threaten him with dire consequences that, whether implemented or not, would affect his son's perception of him for the remainder of his life. Patrick went to his grave convinced that his son was doomed to a life of being "Poor John"—and John eventually went to his grave alone, without family present, leaving behind, for all eternity, a needlessly fractured relationship with his father.

Of all the mistakes that parents make in life, none are more poignant than the ones that could have been repaired by a few well-chosen words of apology.

Nurturing By Any Other Name

Was John O'Hara's dad a nurturing parent? By today's standards, the answer would probably be no. However, by the standards of that time, he would have been considered nurturing. The *Random House Dictionary of the English Language* defines nurturing as providing "nourishment, support, encouragement, etc.," during childhood.

Patrick O'Hara did all that—and more—for his son. He gave him his most heartfelt advice. He supported him. He helped him enter a career of his choosing. At the end of his life, when, with his final breath, he uttered "poor John" to his son, it could be interpreted as either dismissive or caring.

What Patrick O'Hara did not do was make his son feel that he could talk to him about the things that concerned him. It is that type of nurturing that psychologists and social workers would like to see fathers dispense in larger doses. When people speak of feminizing fathers, they usually mean increasing verbal communication between father and son. John O'Hara grew up with the feeling that something was missing in his life. He later explored that void to great benefit in his novels.

Highly charged words such as feminized and androgynous, when used by mothers or psychologists, do not persuade fathers to be more nurturing with their children. A better way of addressing the issue is to be more specific in the requests that are made of fathers. Consider the following exchange between a divorced mother and father:

"Ed, I wish you were more nurturing with little Eddie."

"What do you mean?"

"You know, more nurturing."

If at that point, Ed does what so many ex-husbands do and merely says, "OK, dear," without having a clue about what she is talking about, then nothing will be resolved. If, on the other hand, he presses her for a more accurate definition, he is more likely to take her advice. "But what do you mean by nurturing?"

"Talk to Eddie more. Spend more time playing with him—you know, take him places with you."

"I can't take him many places with me because I'm at work all day, but I can talk to him more—and play with him more. I like doing that anyway."

"Thank you."

CHAPTER 8

Remarriage:
Curse or Salvation?

Whether a mother has lost her husband to death or divorce, one of the most troubling dilemmas she ponders is over finding a replacement husband and father for her son.

Does she need a replacement husband for emotional and financial reasons? Does her son need a replacement father in order to have a male role model?

If the answers to those questions are yes, how soon should she start dating again—and how will it affect her son? Those are weighty questions to ponder on top of everything else, because whether she is widowed or divorced, she still has to deal with her grief and anger over her loss, grandparents who may or may not be supportive, and an altered financial situation that may require relocation and hardship. If the answers to those questions are no, then what comes next?

More than half the women who lose their husbands to divorce marry within five years, thus creating an ever-growing pool of children living with stepfathers. One of the great myths of single parenting is that remarriage is good for the children. In truth, one of the worst reasons for a woman to remarry is to give her son a stepfather. Studies indicate that sons raised in homes with stepfathers exhibit the same dysfunctional symptoms as sons raised by the mother alone. In most cases, providing a fatherless son with a stepfather offers few benefits to the child, can cause real problems for him, and, at best, only maintains the status quo.

That may be because men, despite their best efforts, have a difficult time developing parental love toward children that are not related to them. There is scientific evidence that parenting may have a genetic

131

foundation, which would explain why stepparents have a difficult time "learning" parental instincts. The fact that a man loves a woman has little or no bearing on his capacity to love her son.

Lucile Duberman, writing in *The Reconstituted Family*, reports that only 53 percent of stepfathers and 25 percent of stepmothers in one study claimed to have "parental feelings" toward their stepchildren, and even fewer professed to "love" them. Those figures coincide with our own clinical experience with stepfathers.

Complicating the efforts of stepfathers to be good replacement parents are the built-in barriers to the process. For starters, it is rare that a son would ever want a replacement father. If his biological father is dead, he will resent anyone who attempts to take his place. He will not buy the argument that a stranger can take his father's place simply because he has an emotional attraction to his mother.

If his biological father is alive, the first question a son will ask his mother and his new stepfather is, "What will happen to my dad?" It is a question that deserves a thoughtful answer. No matter what his age at the time of the mother's remarriage, she should give him credit for having his own perspective. The fact that she can replace the biological father with another man and offer him the same love and affection she gave the biological father does not mean that the son can react the same way. The man the mother no longer loves or respects is the same man the son will love and respect forever.

We are not saying that widowed or divorced mothers with children should not remarry. She may have deep emotional or financial needs that remarriage can address and it may be in her best interests to remarry.

What we are saying is that mothers should never remarry solely for the sake of the children, for it will invariably cause problems, especially for sons. Those problems have no bearing on how good or compassionate or loving the stepfather is, or how hard he works to win the hearts of the children.

If his expectation is to replace the biological father, he will encounter stiff opposition and he may ultimately find dissatisfaction with the marriage. It is a primary reason why the failure rate for second marriages in which there are children is almost twice the failure rate of second marriages in which there are no children.

Tips on Remarriage

Know your odds. The optimal time for a mother to remarry is while her children are still of pre-school age. The older the children are at the time of remarriage, the more resistant they will be accepting a stepfather. Adolescent sons usually can be counted on to resist the addition of a replacement father; exceptions can occur in cases where the sons have known the stepfather for several years prior to the marriage.

Consider creative alternatives. Some mothers may not want to hear this, but we think that the responsibilities they have to their children supersede the responsibilities they have to themselves. If the mother of a school-age boy has met the man of her dreams—and does not want to lose either him or her son—perhaps she should postpone marriage, maintain separate households, and work to establish her love interest as a non-parental role model for her son. If that happens, there is a good possibility that the son will be more accepting of a joined household. If the mother's fear is that she must marry the man to hold onto him, then that is evidence enough that the marriage would not stand much of a chance.

Humane vs. parental love. We have all seen children we thought were lovable. We are so programmed to be protective of children, even those we have never met, that we would not hesitate to intercede on their behalf if they were in danger. That type of humane love is culturally induced, subject to logic, and conditional upon the circumstances. It is different from parental love, which is unconditional, instinctive and not subject to logic, and wholly unrelated to circumstance.

Mothers, if you remarry, the best your son may get from your spouse is humane love. Don't go into a second marriage with the expectation that your husband will replace your son's father as a role model, because that probably won't happen. Once again, there are exceptions in which sons form deep emotional attachments to loving stepfathers. It's just not the norm. It is not something you can count on.

Dealing with Superdad. One of the hardest things that mothers and stepfathers face is the fact that sons will continue to love their fathers, regardless of the father's character, intelligence, or economic status. The stepfather can be a deacon in the church, possess several college degrees and be a millionaire, but his stepson will always see him as inferior to his biological father. If the son's father is dead, he will idealize him to the point of sainthood. We can't tell you how many times we have heard stepfathers complain, "His real dad is not half the man I am, yet I can do no right in his eyes." That is a common complaint from stepfathers about their stepsons. We have no advice that will make stepsons love their stepfathers equally with their fathers, but we can offer a tip that, if followed, will help improve their relationship with their stepson:

Never let speak ill of his father. On the contrary, stepfathers should go out of their way to find good things to say about the father, to the point of praising him when it is justified. Divorced mothers often have unresolved conflicts with their son's father and can be forgiven for occasionally losing their perspective; stepfathers have no such excuse and do so at their peril since sons are more forgiving of their mothers than they are of their stepfathers.

Mothers, look before you leap. Studies show that children are more likely to be sexually and physically abused by boyfriends and stepfathers than by natural fathers. In the case of sexual abuse, some stepfathers are attracted to marriage because of the potential it offers for sexual gratification with the mother's children.

Canadian psychologists Margo Wilson and Martin Daly conducted a study in Hamilton, Ontario in which they compared preschoolers who lived with a stepparent to those who lived with both natural parents. They found that preschoolers who lived with one natural parent and one stepparent were forty times more likely to become child abuse victims as children who lived with both natural parents.

Based on their original research and review of other studies they concluded that "stepparenthood per se remains the single most powerful risk factor for child abuse that has yet been identified."

Before marriage, mothers with sons should be alert to inappropriate behavior on the part of the would-be stepfather and exert caution toward men who have had a series of failed relationships with women who have sons.

We don't provide you with the "bad news" of remarriage to frighten you away, but rather to educate you on what to look for and avoid. Stepfamilies can work out well for everyone involved as long as the expectations are not over-inflated. We have personal knowledge of many sons that had happy, fulfilling relationships with their stepfathers, but we realize that they are the exception.

If you are a single mother with a son who is contemplating remarriage, the best advice we can offer you is to not be disappointed if your husband is rejected as a role model by your son. It is not the end of the world. Your son did not choose his biological father (you did!)—but he will choose his own role models. Accept that the man you have selected for a stepfather may not be a suitable role model for your son. If that is the case, you will increase the odds for a successful marriage by finding a male role model for your son **in addition** to his stepfather.

Don't despair because of the statistics on stepfathers. Instead, learn what you need to know to make your son the exception that everyone talks about. Someone has to be the exception. Why not your son?

When Mothers Don't Remarry

Marriage is not for everyone. Mothers who decide not to remarry do so for a variety of reasons—unhappiness in the first marriage, fear of re-experiencing the trauma of divorce or death, financial independence, and a conviction that a second marriage would not be good for her children.

Whether mothers with sons remarry or not, they have a responsibility to find suitable male role models for their sons. She should put the same energy, research and creativity in finding a male role model for her son that she devotes to buying a new car or preparing a presentation at work. Underlying those efforts must be an understanding that no matter how much she loves her son, no matter how much she might be able to teach him about traditional male activities, she can never be a male role model for him.

Suitable male role models can be found in the extended family—maternal or paternal uncles and brothers, for example—or at the mother's place of work, or in the church, temple, or synagogue. We recommend starting with the extended family since that offers the most suitable choices. Talk to brothers, brothers-in-law, cousins and uncles. Explain your needs to them and why their help is so important.

They may not understand what you are asking, practically speaking, so be sure to be specific. Tell them you would like for them to spend time with your son by playing games and sports with him, taking him on outings such as ball games or hunting or fishing, and inviting him on "guy thing" trips such as servicing the car or shopping for boats or hunting bows or fishing tackle.

If you cannot find a suitable male role model within your extended family, consider the fathers of your son's friends. Once again, remember that men are not good at identifying hints, so thoroughly explain what it is that you have in mind.

If neither of the above possibilities produces a suitable role model, then you can try your luck at the church or temple that you attend. Unfortunately, this may actually be a riskier pool since it offers greater potential for problems. As we have seen in recent years, particularly in the sex-abuse scandals associated with Catholic priests, religious organizations sometimes attract pedophiles that use religion as means of ensnaring children. Not everyone who goes to church is worthy of your trust, and you must use as much caution approaching individuals from that pool of role-model prospects as you would any other group. Just because a man is employed by a church that does not mean that he is a saint. He may be just the opposite.

Another possibility is to approach males that you come into contact at work. If you approach someone in that environment, you should choose someone who is married and has children of his own. You should make it clear that you have no romantic interest in him and that the request is being made only in the best interests of your son.

Also worthy of consideration is Big Brothers Big Sisters, a worldwide youth-service organization that screens and matches adult volunteer mentors with school-age children from single-parent families. Big Brothers Big Sisters serves thousands of children in more than five thousand communities in the United States. If this is your choice, you simply enroll your child in the program and wait to hear from the organization. The volunteer that is assigned to your son will be screened for unhealthy motives and matched according to the volunteer's preferences for the type of child he wishes to mentor.

Danger: Proceed with Caution

Although it is essential that mothers of sons without fathers find role models for their children, it is equally important that they screen the men they have chosen. Child predators cannot be weeded out based on some preconceived idea of how they look. In fact, they often look just like the man next door. They often have responsible jobs and families of their own. They are sometimes leaders in their communities. Few pedophiles actually look creepy.

With that in mind, we have prepared a list of red-flag warning signs and problem areas that are consistent with pedophilic leanings in adult males. If you detect the presence of any of the following, you should reconsider that individual as a potential mentor for your son:

*   *   *

He should have a significant other. It matters less whether it is a man or a woman, only that he has a significant-other adult in his life. He should also have a reasonably successful history of relationships with adults. Some mothers feel uncomfortable turning their sons over to homosexual mentors. If that is a concern for you, then you should listen to what your heart tells you. However, you should know that homosexual men are no more likely to be pedophiles than are heterosexual men. A much greater indicator of potential sex abuse is the lack of a significant other. Pedophiles gravitate to children because they have a history of failed relationships with adults. They idealize children by anointing them with the innocence they have lost in their own lives. Of course, there are millions of men in America who are temporarily without significant others. That does not make them pedophiles, but it does make them less than ideal if they envision your son as a substitute for a significant other.

He should not have a history of sexual abuse. It goes without saying that someone who has been charged or convicted of sexually abusing a child should not be chosen as your son's mentor. But it is also important that you not chose someone who has himself been abused as a child. One of the more insidious aspects of child abuse is the fact that abused children often grow up to become abusers themselves. To find out if your prospective mentor has been abused, talk to him about child abuse in general. A proper response would be for him to voice sympathy for abuse victims. An improper response would be for him to say something like, "Children are so innocent." Another red flag would be if he voiced a special understanding of abuse victims (unless, of course, he is a social worker or psychologist who has dealt professionally with abuse victims). If indirect questioning does not produce results, then ask him outright if he has ever been abused as a child. If he says yes, sympathize with him, but then move on to the next candidate. That may sound cold, but your focus should be on protecting your child, not treating adult abuse victims. Leave that to the professionals.

He should not display inappropriate symbols. Beware of men who wear neckties with cartoon characters, men who have stuffed animals in their home, single men who have converted their lawns into playgrounds, or men who have photographs on their walls of children to whom they are not related. Pedophiles use those symbols of childhood to attract victims and to make them feel at ease. It is not so much the cartoon characters, as it is the circumstance under which the necktie is worn that should concern you. Apply this caution to strangers, not to the uncle that shows up for a holiday dinner with a cartoon necktie.

He should not display inappropriate behavior. You want your son's mentor to have a good rapport with him, but you do not want him to be physical with him. It is one thing for a biological father to run his fingers through his son's hair, to tickle him and roll on the floor with him, or to engage in playful behavior such as squirting him with a water hose or wrestling with him, but that same behavior would be inappropriate for a mentor.

He should be comfortable talking about his brothers and sisters. This is a key area of concern. Men who have been abused as children— or have abused children as adults—often have a difficult time discussing their siblings. We won't go into the reasons for that here, but suffice it to say that they have a difficult time remembering their names and ages, they seem at a loss to tell you where they live or what they do for a living, and they often try to change the subject. Ask lots of questions about siblings and back away from him as a potential mentor if he has a difficult time responding.

Anyone can become a pastor, youth minister, or music director. They are not subjected to psychological screening, lie detectors or thorough background checks. If this is the pool from which you would like to find your son's mentor, then use all of the screening guidelines offered here. Pedophiles are attracted to church youth-group organizations because they feel it offers them a degree of immunity from detection since it provides them with a "man of God" image. The vast majority of men involved in youth ministries is there for the right reasons, but keep in mind that it only takes one "wrong reason" to ruin your son's life. Just be alert.

He should be comfortable talking to you about your son. Panic attacks can occur when heterosexual men engage in conversation with a woman they find attractive, and they can occur when homosexual men talk to men they find attractive. The same type of phenomenon occurs when pedophiles discuss children to whom they are attracted. You will not be able to detect all the physical symptoms of a panic attack— increased heart rate and respiration—but you can be alert to increased sweating and increased hand movements to the face, along with apparent blushing. The most telling symptom will be the individual's sudden need for flight. He may stand up, while you are sitting down, and he may pace about the room and then busy himself watering a plant or lighting a cigarette or peering out the window, all done to avoid eye contact with you. In other instances, he may request permission to leave the room by saying, "I really need to go to the bathroom—do you mind if I answer that question when I return?" Use your maternal instincts: if he has a hard time "sitting still," as your son does when he wants to flee your company, you should move on to the next candidate.

*　　*　　*

Locating a male role model for you son will require a lot of hard work on your part, but it will all be worth it in the end—and it may end up literally saving your son's life. You may think it is unfair that you cannot be both mother and father to your son. You may think it is unfair that we have given you guidelines that seem to discriminate against people on the basis of past life experiences.

You should keep in mind that it is your responsibility to be as discriminating as possible on your son's behalf. It is wrong in so many ways to use him to try to change society. Just remember that the purpose in all this is to help your son adjust to an imperfect society, not to use your son to change society.

CHAPTER 9

When Fatherlessness Leads to Illness

Beatle Ringo Starr, an only son, was three years of age when his father abandoned him and his mother. As a result, they moved into the home with his father's parents, where they lived for quite some time. When Ringo was six, his appendix burst and he became very ill with peritonitis. During his one-year stay at the hospital, his mother was told on three different occasions that he would be dead by morning.

After Ringo's release from the hospital his mother was fearful of sending him back to school, where he might be injured by more robust students, so she kept him home for another two years, establishing him as the "little man of the house."

She had the best of intentions—keeping her son out of harm's way. The nightmare that every mother fears is having a doctor say that her son does not have long to live. Ringo's mother heard that phrase on three different occasions! Just imagine what that must have been like the second time she heard it . . . and then the third time!

Ringo's mother blamed his father, because in her mind her son's health problems would never have occurred if he had not abandoned the family. Because she kept him out of school for two years, he didn't learn to read until he was nine, which made him even more insecure around his peers. Not surprisingly, he was sickly throughout his early childhood, encountering one health problem after another.

When he was thirteen, his mother made a radical change in their family by remarrying, an act that instantly demoted him as the "little man of the house." She was hopeful that her new husband would replace

141

the void in her son's life and provide him with the father that he so desperately needed. It didn't work out that way.

Shortly after his mother's remarriage, Ringo developed pleurisy (he says it developed into tuberculosis) and he was returned to the hospital, where he remained for an entire year. When he returned home, he went to school only about a year before dropping out at the age of fifteen.

Ringo felt a great deal of anger toward his father for abandoning him, and his feelings toward his mother were mixed because of her remarriage. Fifteen is a young age to conclude that you have no proper place in life—not as a son, not as a student, not as a boy entering adulthood. If Ringo had not discovered his remarkable talent for music, his story might have had a much different ending. The fact that he was able to make music by striking out with his hands, pounding his frustrations into his drums with a socially accepted level of aggressiveness literally saved his life.

Even so, Ringo's health problems continued into adulthood. He was hospitalized for stomach problems on several occasions and during one episode doctors removed several feet of his intestine. Not surprisingly, alcoholism also became a problem for him.

Only in later years, did it all make sense to him. "I have no real memories of my dad. I only saw him probably five times after he left, and I never really got on with him because I'd been brainwashed by my mother about what a pig he was," he said in The Beatles Anthology. "I felt angry that he left. And I felt really angry later on, going through therapy in rehab, when I came to look at myself and got to know my feelings, instead of blocking them all out. For me, I felt I'd dealt with it when I was little. I didn't understand that really I had been blocking my anger out."

Ringo's appendicitis was not caused by his status as a son without a father, and his first extended stay in the hospital was due to the fact that he injured himself falling out of bed, but subsequent health problems with his lungs and stomach may have been due in part to the emotional turmoil he felt over his fatherlessness.

In retrospect, it is easy to say that Ringo's mother was overprotective, but at the time she felt she was fighting for his life. She cried out to the medical community for help—and Ringo apparently was given adequate medical care—but no one had enough information about fatherlessness to connect the dots to his health problems.

Ringo certainly made a success out of his life. We will never know whether that success was due to the hardships he endured—or whether it occurred in spite of them. The one thing we do know is that his mother was highly motivated to take care of him. If she had had the information then that is available now about sons without fathers, his childhood would have been a different experience.

Sons at Greater Risk of Certain Ailments

Compared to children living with a father, fatherless children experience more accidental injury, asthma, frequent headaches, and speech defects, according to the *Journal of Marriage and Family.* Overall health also is affected by the absence of a father in the home. In a 1995 survey of children under seventeen, the U.S. Department of Health and Human Services found that 55 percent of the children found to be in good health lived with both biological parents, while only 42 percent lived with single mothers.

Recent studies indicate that there is both a genetic and a cultural basis for how individuals react to pain. Boys and girls have different reactions. The genetic difference is based on estrogen, a chemical that increases the availability of pain-numbing endorphins in females and allows them to be more tolerant of the pain associated with illness than males. The cultural factor is the way in which males are taught from early childhood that "big boys don't cry" when they feel pain.

Even though they feel pain more acutely than their mothers and sisters, little boys are taught to "tough it out" by not complaining about their discomfort. In father-absent homes, mothers evaluate injuries to their sons in terms of their own pain threshold to similar injuries, which means that they tend to under-evaluate their son's discomfort. Without meaning to do so, parents sometimes teach their sons to ignore the early symptoms of disease, for fear of being called a "sissy," thus increasing the likelihood that their illnesses will require more extensive treatment.

A Swedish study, published in 2003 in *The Lancet,* a British medical journal, found that children with single parents were twice as likely as children in intact families to develop serious psychiatric illnesses such as severe depression or schizophrenia. Although schizophrenia has a genetic foundation and can occur without regard to parenting considerations, research suggests that it may be triggered by family stresses. The implications for mothers of sons without fathers are obvious in families in which there is a history of schizophrenia.

An Israeli study found that children of divorced parents are seven times more likely to suffer from depression in adult life than children of similar age and background whose parents have not divorced. The researchers found that the loss of a parent to divorce was more likely to cause depression than a loss through death. Concluded Bernard Lerer of the Biological Psychiatric Unit at Hadassah Hospital in Jerusalem: "The earlier the separation occurred, the more likely it was to have had an influence."

Of course, there are other reasons for childhood depression. A 1997 study found that families of depressed children were five times as likely as those of non-depressed children to have someone in the family who suffers from depression. That would seem to indicate a genetic predisposition for depression.

Sons without fathers are at risk for depression without the presence of a family history of depression, but if that history is present, particularly in the mother, the odds of depression developing as a result of parental separation increase dramatically. Studies have shown that depression in boys is correlated with depression in mothers more so than with depression in fathers. A mother that is depressed because she has lost her husband through death or divorce is more likely to contribute to her son's depression than a mother that has not had those life experiences.

Information like this is helpful to both parents and physicians. All too often, sons without fathers are blamed for having too many accidents that require first-aid attention. They are admonished to "be more careful" or they are told outright that they are "stupid" for having so many cuts and scrapes.

Parents sometimes get angry with children who display symptoms of depression because they think the children are hiding something from them, or because they interpret the child's behavior as a rejection of them as a parent. In those situations, parental anger only fuels the depression.

Imagine that you are a 10-year-old boy who feels sadness over the loss of his father, emotions that you cannot articulate to yourself much less to another person, and powerlessness at a new school, where you feel like an unwanted outsider—and your mother, who is twice your size, stands over you, angrily chastising you because of your sadness and threatening you with a loss of the very privileges that make you feel better unless you "straighten up" and show a better attitude!

From that perspective, you can understand how a boy would perceive his mother's well-meaning admonitions as veiled threats to deprive him of her love and attention. It is the type of parenting that could drive the child further into depression.

We aren't suggesting that mothers lose sleep over fears that they are ruining their sons' health—most boys bypass or overcome the mental and physical ailments associated with being a son without a father (just look at the successful way Ringo Starr turned his life around)—but we think that an awareness of worst-case scenarios is helpful in reminding parents that there is a cause-effect influence at work in their parenting decisions. Usually, that awareness is enough to keep mothers alert to potential problems.

The most important thing a mother can do is to pay attention to her son's ailments. Is there a pattern? Does he get asthma after visits with his father? Does he get depressed after the mother has arguments with his father? Is he spending too much time alone in his room? Look for patterns to his asthma attacks, his headaches, speech problems and his injuries—and then stay on top of them.

Sending your son to a physician is not enough. A physician can prescribe medications for most of the ailments we have mentioned, but unless he is aware of a pattern to your son's ailments, he or she is at a disadvantage. One of the worst mistakes that a mother can make is to assume that someone else, some good soul further down the road, will intervene to provide her son with a happy and successful life. If only real life were like that: In most cases, it is now or never.

We heard a distraught mother once comment that, "I took my son to the doctor—what more could I have done?" Simply taking a child to the doctor is not enough. Doctors are not mind readers. They make diagnoses based on what they see and hear, and, in the case of children, what they are told by the parents. It is essential that the parents of sons without fathers educate themselves on the diseases and ailments that are more likely to strike their sons.

Since depression is one of the most common ailments associated with fatherlessness, it is important for mothers to acquaint themselves with the warning signs.

Early Warning Signs of Depression

You should be concerned if your child:

- sleeps late and has a hard time waking up. He may also wake up early and not be able to go back to sleep.

- becomes unusually irritable without apparent explanation and lose his temper over minor matters.

- complains of a loss of energy and says they just aren't interested in the things they used to be interested in. They show no interest in inviting friends over to play games, listen to music or watch television; instead, they do those activities alone.

- They complain of a series of vague aches and pains for which there is no apparent cause (i.e. no swelling, bruising, cuts, redness, signs of insect bites or stings, fever, bleeding, etc.).

- If you receive a telephone call from his teacher, who says that your son is falling behind. The teacher asks if anything is wrong.
- If your child's mood swings between over-excitement and apparent sadness
- If he loses interest in religious activities, or gains a sudden passion for them.

* * *

Parents should not be overly concerned if their child displays one or two of the above symptoms. However, if the child exhibits three or more of the symptoms, they should have the child evaluated by a professional.

Parents should be especially alert if depression runs in their family, or if one of the parents is being treated for depression. In *Understanding Teenage Depression,* Dr. Maureen Empfield concluded that between 50 to 75 percent of depressed children have mothers who suffer from the same illness. "The mothers of depressed teenagers have particularly high rates of depression," she observed. "There is less of a correlation with fathers' rates."

If the mother is experiencing the symptoms of depression herself, it is important that she seek professional help—for her son's sake, if for no other reason, because if she does not, her depression could contribute to his depression. Those feelings of hopelessness and despair that she experiences do not mean that she is crazy and unfit to care for her son. Divorced and widowed mothers have a right to have those feelings. All mothers in that situation have those feelings at one time or another.

Therapists can make a difference, so it is important to seek their help. If it turns out that there is a medical reason for the depression, such as a chemical imbalance, it is essential that it be treated with medication by a physician who specializes in depression.

CHAPTER 10

What Parents Need to Know About Adult Sons without Fathers

Without informed help from their mothers, most Unfriendly World sons see the world as a dangerous place that must be battled on every front. Danger lurks around every corner. They are easily angered and slow to forgive; they are pessimistic about relationships and they tend to be loners, even if married; they overreact when criticized by strangers, co-workers, employers or family members. They distrust consensus and they gravitate toward radical political movements that challenge established authority.

All this is of concern to women for two reasons: 1) sons raised without fathers are someday going to be husbands and fathers—and many of their same ways of thinking and acting will continue into adulthood, which means that it presents a lifelong challenge to their spouses; and 2) mothers of fatherless sons often remarry men who were themselves sons without fathers, which means that they must deal with many of the same problems, only on an adult level. Women should pack this information away in their survival kit!

Heterosexual relationships present a special problem for Unfriendly World adults. Males who grow up in homes in which they were never able to observe the various ways that men and women communicate and resolve conflict, often find themselves at a loss when they enter into relationships with members of the opposite sex. Conflict resolution between men and women is learned behavior, not genetic, so sons that never see male/female conflict resolution at home enter adult life at a disadvantage.

They try to resolve conflicts with the same techniques they used with their mothers and playmates. Since as children they rarely won disputes with their mothers, the tendency is for them to assume the parental role used by their mothers when they become adults. They become "mothers" instead of boyfriends and husbands. They talk down to their wives or girlfriends and expect them to do what they say because that is the way it worked when they were growing up. Mothers *always* won the arguments because there was no one of equal status to debate the issue with them.

A common complaint heard from the wives of sons without fathers is that they are inept negotiators. "Ed doesn't know how to negotiate for what he wants," explained one distraught woman who had persuaded her husband to attend counseling. "It's always his way—or no way! When I talk to him, he can look me squarely in the face and still not hear a word I am saying. If I disagree with him about something, you would think it was the end of the world. He can't handle criticism."

Unfriendly World men do not travel in packs. They typically have one or two close male friends and numerous female friends. When they marry, they do best when they marry a woman with whom they have a strong friendship. Bill Clinton and Tom Cruise are good examples of Unfriendly World men who have more female friends than male friends, and who build marriages based on strong friendship attractions.

Unfriendly World men often attempt to "mother" their girlfriends and wives. Women find that flattering at first, but what seemed like adoring attention in the beginning sometimes becomes oppressive and a threat to the relationship.

If women challenge their mothering attempts, Unfriendly World men interpret that as a criticism. Unfriendly World men consider anyone who sees the universe as friendly as foolish. They look on in awe and sometimes disgust as their friendly-world friends undertake everyday decisions as if they are going to live forever. Unfriendly World adults have a problem accepting the concept of forever. They know from experience, whether because of divorce or death or a father who was never in the picture, that life is mostly a disappointing series of rejections and disappointments. They know that bad things are waiting just around the corner, ready to take away what they value.

One of the most troublesome characteristics of Unfriendly World men is their tendency to overact. If attacked physically, they are likely to fight to the death. It is not enough for them to disable their opponents; they want to destroy them. If attacked for their views or opinions, they are likely to feel a surge of anger that will typically be displayed by a red face, raised voice, elevated blood pressure and respiration, and clinched fists. For that reason, they do not make good negotiators. They are quick to say things they later regret and they are quick to walk out of meetings.

As we have said throughout this book, the ranks of fatherless sons are filled with exceptions, individuals who beat the odds. That is why we wrote this book: To move more sons into the exceptional category. Being a son without a father is not a terminal illness. It is a condition that responds to treatment.

Mothers should not assume that their sons and husbands will exhibit all of the characteristics we have listed in this chapter, but they can be certain that all sons without fathers will exhibit some of these characteristics at some point in their lives. Knowing why they act the way they do is important to maintain a healthy relationship.

'It Takes One to Know One'

Born to Russian Jewish immigrants, actor Kirk Douglas became an Unfriendly World son under unusual circumstances. When he was thirteen, his mother decided to move the family, consisting of him and six sisters, to a better neighborhood, but his father stayed behind, stubbornly refusing to budge from their old house.

"If only Pa had said, 'Stay with me, son,'" Douglas later wrote in his autobiography. "But Pa said nothing. He stormed out of the house, to O'Shaughnessey's or Boggi's saloon, a world where men drank and forgot their problems. And he left me in a world of women. I left Pa . . . pacing the kitchen, and went off with my six sisters and my mother. And I felt as if I had been circumcised again."

As traumatic as that event was—in some ways it was like witnessing the death of his father—Douglas had felt alienated from his father for quite some time. He was outwardly affectionate toward neither his wife nor his children. A ragman by trade, he saw his primary role as that of provider. He worked hard, and felt that the family was his wife's responsibility. He was so distant toward her that, later in life, Douglas could not remember him ever calling her by her name. It was always "Hey you!" Nor could he recall his father ever having a conversation with his wife or children.

"I loved my father but I hated him, too," Douglas wrote. "He was strong. He was a man. I didn't know what I was. But I wanted to be accepted by him, to be given a pat on the back."

Many years later, when he was a successful Hollywood actor, Douglas found marriage difficult. No one had ever shown him how to be a father and a husband. Once, while Douglas having an argument with his wife, Diana, their son Michael walked into the room. They immediately stopped arguing, but Michael could tell from their faces what was happening and he burst into tears. It was at that point that they decided that staying together "for the sake of the children" was not going to work, so they filed for divorce. Diana took their two sons with her and moved to New York.

Later, when Douglas went to visit his sons, six-year-old Michael burst into tears as soon as he walked in the door. He found the visit awkward. "I wanted so much to create with Michael and Joel the relationship I had missed with my father," Douglas wrote. "I wanted them to know I cared. Still, there was a wall between us. Maybe they felt that I had abandoned them. We never discussed it. It's hard to be a father."

When he was older, Michael was sent to a boys' school in Connecticut. After graduation, he enrolled at the University of California, where he followed in his father's footsteps and majored in drama. As Michael pursued a successful career as an actor and film producer, he married and had a son named Cameron. The marriage lasted for twenty-two years, thus giving Michael the opportunity to *reverse the son-without-a-father cycle that had begun with his father. Cameron came of age with a father in the home, something that had not happened with either Michael or his father. After his divorce, Michael married actress Catherine Zeta-Jones, with whom he has had two children—a girl named Carys and a boy named Dylan.*

In the late 1980s, while Michael was promoting his film Fatal Attraction, he visited his father at his Los Angeles home. During a pause in the conversation, Kirk asked his son something that had been on his mind for a long time. He asked him how he had been as a father.

Michael told him that he had been "loony," always anxious over his films.

"I looked at Michael—the lines of fatigue around his eyes, the tension in his jaw," Kirk later wrote. "I started to laugh. Michael swung around and stared at me. 'What's funny?'

'I must have been a lot like you are right now.'

Michael broke into a grin and kissed his father.

"It takes one to know one."

And so it goes with sons without fathers. It takes one to know one, and it takes an extraordinary son to break the cycle. Michael thus far has shown uncommon devotion to his children with Catherine. If he succeeds in preventing his youngest son, Dylan, from ever feeling the pain of rejection that he felt as a child, and that his father before him felt, then he will have accomplished a great thing. Too bad they don't give Oscars for that.

Back to the Future
Fathers and Sons

If the father of an Unfriendly World son is himself an Unfriendly Word son, it creates special problems and challenges for him, but it also offers rare opportunities for understanding, growth and healing.

One of the hardest things for the Unfriendly World father to understand about his Unfriendly World son is that they share the same approach to life. That realization took decades for Kirk and Michael Douglas, yet when it finally happened, it could be explained with

Michael's observation: "It takes one to know one." That level of self-realization is what every father and son should work toward, for it will be difficult for either to find inner peace until it is reached. Sometimes, it does not occur until the father is a senior and the son is in middle age.

By the time an Unfriendly World son grows up, marries and starts a family of his own, he convinces himself that he has come to terms with his past. It is not until his family falls apart—and he casts his own son out into an unfriendly word—that he realizes that he is destined to re-live his past through his son.

What Fathers Share with their Sons

There were times when Norman felt like an observer in his own life, never more so than when he and Lisa married after a brief courtship while still in college. Lisa was several years younger, and while she had not lost her father to death, as Norman had done as a small child, she did lose him to divorce when she was eleven.

An only child, she grew up in a home with an abusive mother; when her father visited, which was seldom, he was always verbally abusive to her. Once he took her to lunch, just the two of them, but the outing was quickly terminated when Lisa accidentally spilled her milk. "That's it," he barked, rising to his feet. "I'm taking you home."

Norman and Lisa forged a strong marriage based on their mutual perception that the world is a treacherous place. Once they left college and entered the workplace, they circled their wagons and avoided contact with other couples. They led an insular life that was built around their emotional needs as a couple and their fears of the outside world.

Three years into the marriage, Lisa got pregnant. Norman was delighted. They both envisioned their unborn child as an integral building block in what they described as their "family unit." However, their excitement turned to despair when Lisa developed a toxic condition that led to a premature birth. During labor, the doctor pulled Norman aside and told him that Lisa's blood pressure was dangerously high and they were unable to reduce it.

"Be prepared for the worst," explained the doctor. "We could lose her."

That didn't happen, though. Lisa gave birth to a six-pound boy they named Norman Jr. By the time they took him home from the hospital they were already calling him Little Norman. It was a name that stuck with him all the way through childhood.

Parenthood was not what either had expected. Little Norman cried during most of his waking hours, a condition that has been correlated with toxic-birth children. Lisa was exhausted by the time Norman got home from work and by the time they went to bed, both were exhausted from the energy they expended caring for Little Norman.

Somehow they muddled through eight more years of marriage. By then, Norman and Lisa no longer thought of themselves as a family unit. They seldom thought of each other at all. It was not a great marriage, but it was not a bad one either, not in the sense that they had violent arguments or pursued secret infidelities.

One day Norman was at work when a deputy sheriff drove up without warning and served him with divorce papers. He was stunned. They had never once discussed a separation or divorce. There was nothing to discuss. Lisa wanted a divorce.

When they told Little Norman, then eight years of age, he stared at them a moment before he spoke.

"Is it because of me?" he asked.

"No," they both told him.

But he did not believe them.

Soon after the divorce, Norman was transferred to another city. He visited with Little Norman twice a month in the beginning, but as the years went by their visits occurred every two or three months and then settled into a summers-only routine that continued all the way though junior high and then high school.

One day, during one of their summer visits, Little Norman asked his father a question: "Mom said you left us because you wanted to marry another woman. Why didn't you marry her?"

Norman was furious.

"That's not true," he said. "Not on any count. I was not involved with another woman—and I didn't leave you. Your mother divorced me."

"That's not what she says."

"I don't know why she would say that. It's not true."

Each summer, all the way into adulthood, Little Norman repeated the same two questions. Nothing Norman said could convince him otherwise. In retrospect, it seems like a small matter, but at the time it was not small to either father or son.

Norman stopped speaking to Lisa after Little Norman asked the question the first second or third time, but as the years went by father and son also stopped talking to each other. On Norman's fiftieth birthday, Little Norman called his dad to wish him a happy birthday. Norman was delighted to hear from his son, but they were no more than ten minutes into the conversation when Little Norman asked, once again, why he had left him and his mother for another woman.

"Damn!" Norman said, slamming down the telephone. "Is there no end to this?"

Norman and Little Norman were trapped in a father-son relationship that neither could escape because they were too much alike to ever see a world with a silver lining. Without professional intervention, their relationship would have gone in circles until one of them died. In therapy they learned to see each other as potential friends instead of enemies— and with a little work they were able to have a fresh start.

Ways Fathers and Sons are Alike

Simmering Anger. This is the primary emotion that all Unfriendly World sons feel throughout life. In the event of a father's death, the anger is usually expressed toward God, for taking the father without regard to the son's needs, and toward the son himself, for a wide range of imagined injustices toward the father. For example, the son may feel that the father would have been spared if only the son had cleaned his room, gone to church more often, or fed the family pet. That anger is compounded if he ever sees his mother in tears because he will see her as an innocent victim.

In divorce, the anger is expressed toward everyone involved, particularly the mother because without all the facts the son may feel that she drove the father away. Children often have a more difficult time dealing with divorce or the imprisonment of a father than they do dealing with the death of a parent. No matter how compassionately or politely that divorce or imprisonment is explained to children, they are devastated and usually spend the remainder of their lives dealing with it.

In the case of Norman and Little Norman, each was handicapped by anger, though for different reasons. Unresolved anger was what destroyed their relationship. The fact that their anger was unreasonable— and at time irrational—made little difference: They reacted to what they felt and lived their lives accordingly.

Loneliness. Sons who have lost their fathers feel a deep sense of loneliness. It is surprising how frequently adult family members fail to understand the intensity with which a child feels the loss of a parent. They tell the child to go outside and play or they admonish him to be quiet and watch television.

Any adult son without a father can attest to the overwhelming sense of loneliness he felt upon the loss. Typically, it will be more intense that what other family members, even the mother, felt. The mother, the grandparents, the aunts and uncles, all have multi-layered lives. They have jobs to go to, organizations to attend, adult friends who will take the time to comfort them. Children are totally dependent on their parents for emotional support. There is nothing in place to replace that support once it is removed, which is why children feel such a greater level of loneliness at such times.

You would think that a father and a son who have faced such loneliness would be able to relate in a nurturing way to each other. Unfortunately, in those situations father and son are like magnets in that when pushed together they repel instead of attract. Without professional mediation, neither is likely to move past that impasse.

The loneliness felt by father and son can be used as a healing tool, but it almost always requires the intervention of a neutral third party that understands the simmering anger that lies behind the loneliness.

Guilt. Fathers sometimes feel guilty about divorces that involve children, even when they are not at fault. They try to rationalize it, depending on the causes of the divorce, by thinking, "She's the one who cheated, not me," or "I can't help it if I fell in love with someone else." Those rationalizations may be circling about in their brain, but they do nothing to lessen the guilt that underlies the actual cause of the divorce. Sons feel guilty because they think their parents would still be together if only they had done something differently. He may think, "Dad (or Mom) would not have fallen in love with someone else if I had not talked back so often (or gotten in trouble in school)," or he may think that since his bad behavior was a subject of frequent arguments between the parents, that he was the reason they broke up.

When the son reaches adulthood, divorce guilt may prevent him from visiting or communicating with his father. He may say to friends, "If my father wants to see me, he will call," but what he is really thinking is that his father has not yet forgiven him for breaking up the marriage. He usually decides to "just give it more time."

By the time the father sees his son reach adulthood his guilt has reached such a point that he has convinced himself that he has not heard from his son because he is unable to forgive him for breaking up the family. He may say to friends, "If my son wants to see me, he will call," or he may say, "If my son expects me to beg for forgiveness, he is mistaken." He decides to give the situation more time to see if it will "work itself out."

Disappointment with Life. A couple of years before his fiftieth birthday, Nobel Prize-winning author William Faulkner wrote, "For some time I have expected, at a certain age, to reach that period [in the early fifties] which most artists seem to reach where they admit at last that there is no solution to life and that it is not, and perhaps never was, worth the living."

Faulkner was writing about the artistic temperament, but he might well have been commenting on Unfriendly World fathers and sons. Disappointment with life is at the deepest core of their being. The older they get, the more disappointed they become, which is why so many Unfriendly World fathers and sons suffer from depression.

It is also why when father and son spend time together, they often walk away from the experience with feelings of emptiness. How could it be otherwise? If neither person thinks that life is worth living, it is unlikely, without professional intervention, that either will find common ground for optimism in their relationship.

Fear of Rejection. Unfriendly World fathers who have experienced rejection are so sensitive to the prospect of future rejection that they sometimes stop taking chances in life. "Why try?" the father may remark. "It always ends the same way. What's the point?"

For sons, the experience is much the same.

"My father left me once, so why should I give him a chance to do it again? If I get close to him, I just know something bad will happen."

It is self-destructive to avoid the person you love simply because you fear they might reject you, but it happens all the time in the Unfriendly World.

One thing we recommend in these situations is that father and son undertake a brief outing together—it could be fishing or golf or any number of outdoor activities—with the understanding that neither is allowed to speak during the entire outing. We urge them to make a game of it. What usually happens is that father and son have a pleasant time participating in an activity that is immune to discussions about blame and the accompanying feelings of rejection.

Because they are successful "doing" something together, they do not end the experience with either person feeling rejected by the other. For their next outing, they should be allowed to discuss non-personal issues such as sports or politics, and so on, until after several outings they are ready to talk to each other about their true feelings.

Attraction to Abused Women. The last thing that Unfriendly World fathers and sons need in life are relationships with a significant others who have a history of abuse or dysfunction, yet they are drawn to such people like moths to a flame. They are attracted to people who have experienced sexual or physical abuse as a child, and they are attracted to adults who have been emotionally bruised by alcoholism or drug addiction.

There are any number of reasons why this happens—genuine sympathy for others who have had disappointments in life, well-concealed feelings of self-loathing and self-destruction that resulted from their own Unfriendly World childhood, or a desire to use the pain of others to combat the loneliness, rejection and disappointment in their own life.

Norman was astonished to discover that every woman he dated after his divorce had a history of sexual abuse. "How do these women find me?" he once complained. The more important question, of course, was "Why am I attracted to them?" Norman never considered that question, until he was forced to address it in therapy.

Little Norman's relationship handicap was his attraction to women with alcohol or drug problems. None of those relationships ever worked out, but that never stopped him from pursuing another one. His behavior was instigated by unresolved feelings of anger toward his mother. Unable to "fix" his parents' lives, he lived out his own life determined to repair the shattered lives of needy women.

Norman and Little Norman often used problems associated with their significant others to postpone dealing with their problems with each other. In those instances, the women were little more than crutches. The women used them. They used the women. Being used became a convenient excuse for father and son to avoid each other.

How Unfriendly World Fathers Relate to Other Males

Perhaps because they grow up in households where the most significant relationships are with females, sons without fathers usually come of age on the crest of a long string of females relationships, whether it is with their mother or their sister or their female neighbors and classmates in pre-school and grammar school.

As adults, sons without fathers continue that tendency to form strong friendships with women, sometimes to the exclusion of male friendships. Tom Cruise is a good example, for despite his public image as a man's man, he puts a higher value on his female friendships. It is rare to see sons without fathers going out on the town with a bunch of guys. They typically have one close male friend and numerous female friends.

This tendency makes for interesting situations among Unfriendly World fathers and sons, and the other males in the family. Unless the grandfathers or the uncles grew up in single-parent families, it is unlikely they will relate to their Unfriendly World grandsons or nephews in the way that they relate to each other. They will probably feel the same affection, but it sometimes will be tempered by an awkward familiarity.

If the divorced grandfather is still living, it may create a situation in which the grandfather may develop a closer bond with his grandson than with his son. That is because neither holds the other responsible for their disappointments in life. Rather, they both blame the father for things that have gone wrong in their lives. The son may blame him for breaking up the family and the grandfather may blame him for causing his mother grief after the divorce. That puts the father in the middle, which is not a surprise to him since he usually has issues with both his father and his son.

It is important that everyone involved avoid the creation of alliances. Sons without fathers are ultra sensitive to the issue of betrayal. Actually, it is the issue of betrayal that most often keeps sons without fathers from enjoying long-term relationships with other males. They might forgive their girlfriend if she flirts with his best friend, but if that situation is reversed, they will sever their relationships with their best friend if he flirts with his girlfriend. It is a double standard, to be for sure, but it reflects a deep-seated belief among sons without fathers, whether conscious or not, that males have a responsibility to honor relationship boundaries.

When Your Sons Are Fathers

Mothers who have raised sons without fathers sometimes experience déjà vu when their sons have sons of their own, especially if the marriage falls apart and the grandsons live with their mother. Grandmother thought she was through with the stresses of raising a son without a father—and it comes back full circle to her, putting her in the position of mothering both her adult son and her grandson.

If you find yourself in that position, there are things you should know.

Your grandson will go through the same emotions experienced by your son. If you do not have a good relationship with your ex-daughter-in-law, you should do everything in your power to improve that relationship for the sake of both your son and your grandson. If you have a good relationship with your ex-daughter-in-law, then you should take advantage of that goodwill to share what you learned about raising a son without a father. With any luck, she will dote on every word—just as long as you refrain from trying to influence her opinion of your son.

When your grandson visits, it will offer you an opportunity to improve on how you raised your son. Play with him, talk to him, encourage his interests in sports, music, painting or writing. Put him in the company of older males whenever possible. Reassure him that his father loves him, and be supportive of his mother's efforts to discipline him. Never speak ill of his mother. Bite your tongue if you feel the urge.

You will have to help your son learn how to relate to his son. You should urge your son to be more nurturing toward his son. Sometimes the best thing that a father can do to build a better relationship with his son is to mimic his ex-wife's behavior toward him. Most likely, she sees herself as the nurturing parent. She offers to do things for her son, whether it is tying his shoelaces or buying him his favorite sneakers. She bandages his nicks and scrapes. She asks if he wants a snack. Those are things that a dad can do with equal success.

Ask your son this: "If you worked with two individuals, one of whom always offered to bring you your coffee, washed your car occasionally, and brought you gifts, and the other of whom never spoke to you unless you spoke to them first, which co-worker would you feel closer to?"

Explain to him that the same principle works with his son.

When his wife wanted to give their son a delicious snack, she didn't ask dad to call him. She called him herself. However, when he was outside playing or upstairs in his room, she asked the dad to call him and he probably said something like, "Get inside (or downstairs) for dinner!" Once the son shuffled to the dinner table, he probably tossed the dad an unappreciative glare, only to have it erased by the soothing voice of his mother, who cooed, "Look what Mom cooked for you tonight!"

Fathers should forget the "strong silent type" role they admired in the 1953 classic film *Shane*. It is not appropriate for their relationship with their son. Alan Ladd, who played the gunfighter with a heart of gold, was strong and silent toward the bad guys, not toward Joey, the little boy who admired him. On the contrary, he played games with Joey and spoke to him as if he were an adult. Fathers who are having problems with their sons should watch *Shane* with them.

Your son would not like it if his friends played the "strong silent type" with him, so you should urge him not to fall into that trap with his son. He should learn from his ex-wife's behavior toward their son. His son bonded with his mother because she addressed his needs and went out of her way to do good things for him.

Perhaps the most powerful thing you can say to your son is to remind him of the things he missed out on because he did not have a father. If your son is in need of a bottom-line slogan, you can go with this one: **Treat your son the way you always wanted to be treated by your father**.

A father's goal should be to elevate his son's view of himself, not to achieve some misguided utopian level of justice in his own life. Your son will feel better about life when his son feels better about life—and probably not before then.

Look for the Silver Lining

If you are the mother, wife or girlfriend of a son without a father who was able to overcome his past and become the exception, then you know that there is a very positive side to this story. Exceptional sons without fathers tend to possess the sort of personal qualities that often lead to success in life. Sons who make it to the other side, so to speak, often emerge as extremely empathetic. You can bring tears to the eyes of Bill Clinton simply by telling him a story about a hard-luck family. He really can feel their pain. That level of empathy is characteristic of sons without fathers that overcome their past.

Brandon was four when his father died. He was raised by his mother and aunt, along with two brothers and a sister, in a household in which everyone had to pitch in to help. While still in grade school he learned to cook, clean the house and do the washing, because—with his mother working as a telephone operator and his aunt operating a beauty parlor—everyone was expected to do their part.

From an early age, Brandon dreamed of becoming a doctor so that he could ease the pain of others. It was the psychological equivalent of immersing himself in sports or music. It surprised no one that he pursued that dream through to its end result. As a physician, he specialized in rehabilitation, an area that allowed him to treat the pain suffered by others. He did not have a father to teach him empathy, but he found it through his mother's and aunt's encouragement to pursue his dream to make a difference in life.

Another quality that exceptional sons without fathers possess is loyalty. You would be hard-pressed to find an exceptional son without a father who is not described as being loyal to the extreme. He will stand by his friends, no matter what, even if it brings pain to himself. Say what you will about Tom Cruise—you may hate his acting, or love it—but he is extremely loyal to his friends and to his children.

Most exceptional sons without fathers are like that. If you are a soldier and you are headed for battle, you will want him at your side. If you are a fireman or a policeman, you will want him as your partner. If you are his wife or his mother and you run into a crisis, you will know that he will stand by you in your time of trouble. How could it be otherwise? Sons without fathers have felt the greatest loss it is possible for a boy to experience. They have survived because of the devotion shown to them by those that love them—and they often feel compelled to repay that debt by being loyal to others.

In the end, mothers of sons without fathers have a choice about what kind of son they will raise. It is our hope that they will take the information in this book and use it to raise an exceptional child.

AUTHORS NOTE

1. All population statistics used in this section, and throughout the book, were obtained from the U. S. Census Bureau.

2. All national statistics involving crime came from the U.S. Department of Justice. The Wisconsin figures correlating juvenile delinquency with father-absent homes came from the Wisconsin Department of Health and Social Services, 1994.

3. We are indebted to Lise Eliot, for sharing her thoughts about early brain development with us in an interview. She is an assistant professor in the department of neuroscience at the Chicago Medical School. Her research has focused on brain plasticity and the neural basis of learning and memory. She has written on the subject in *What's Going on in There? How the Brain and Mind Develop in the First Five Years of Life.*

ACKNOWLEDGMENTS

Mardi Allen would like to thank librarian and friend Margueritte Ransom, who diligently searched for books and articles for this project; my family who always believes in me far beyond my abilities; Billye Bob Currie who during a practicum experience encouraged me to learn and grow as a therapist; Paul Cotten and John Lipscomb who believed in me and pushed me to succeed early in my career; Steve Szukula for his supervision during my internship at Primary Children's Medical Center; Sam Goldstein at the Neurology, Learning and Behavior Center who was a great mentor to me during my post-doctoral residency training; Austin, Matthew and Brandon who thought it was cool for me to write this book; and my sweet canine girls, Mattie and Allie.

James L. Dickerson would like to thank Sharon Gary, a Memphis psychologist and friend; the late David Rice, a dedicated social worker and family therapist who has made a difference in the lives of countless children, and his creative wife, Debra; the late Ross Fenemore, who devoted a lifetime to protecting the children in his community; the late Jean Gardner, a social crusader who felt the pain of everyone who came into her life; and the late Florene Brownell, a nurse who never met a baby she did not love.

Bibliography

BOOKS

Ackerman, Marc J. and Andrew Kane. *Psychological Experts in Divorce, Personal Injury and Other Civil Actions.* New York: Wiley & Sons, 1993.

Ainsworth, M.D. *Patterns of Attachment.* Hillsdale, N.J. :Erlbaun, 1978.

Aries, Philippe. *Centuries of Childhood: A Social History of Family Life.* New York: Vintage, 1965.

Armstrong, Louis. *Louis Armstrong: In His Own Words.* New York: Oxford University Press, 1999.

Bachrach, Arthur J., and Gardner Murphy, eds. *An Outline of Abnormal Psychology.* New York: Modern Library, 1954.

Barron-Cohen, Simon. *The Essential Difference: The Truth About the Male and Female Brain.* New York: Perseus, 2003.

Beatles. *The Beatles Anthology.* San Francisco: Chronicle Books, 2000.

Bergreen, Laurence. *Louis Armstrong: An Extravagant Life.* New York: Broadway Books, 1997.

Biddulph, Steve. *Raising Boys.* Berkeley, Calif.: Celestial Arts.

Biller, Henry. *Fathers and Families: Paternal Factors in Child Development.* Westport, Conn.: Auburn House, 1993.

Biller, Henry, and Dennis Meredith. *Father Power.* New York: David McKay, 1974.

Biller, Henry B., and Robert J. Trotter. *The Father Factor: What You Need to Know to Make a Difference.* New York: Pocket Books.

Blankenhorn, David. *Fatherless America: Confonting Our Most Urgent Social Problem.* New York: Harper Perennial, 1995.

Blau, Theodore H. *The Psychologist as Expert Witness.* New York: John Wiley & Sons, 1988.

Blotner, Joseph, ed. *Selected Letters of William Faulkner.* New York: Random House, 1977.
Bower, T. *Development in Infancy.* San Francisco: Freeman, 1981.

Brazelton, T.B. *The Infant Neonatal Assessment Scale.* Philadelphia: Lippincott, 1984.

Burns, Ailsa, and Cath Scott. *Mother-Headed Families and Why They Have Increased.* Hillsdale, New Jersey: Lawrence Erlbaum Associates, 1994.

Caldwell, Bettye M., and Henry N. Ricciuti, eds. *Child Development and Social Policy.* Volume 3. Chicago: University of Chicago Press, 1973.

Canfield, Ken R. *The 7 Secrets of Effective Fathers.* Wheaton, Illinois: Tyndale House, 1992.

Cramer, Richard Ben. *Joe DiMaggio: The Hero's Life.* New York: Simon & Schuster, 2000.

Crews, Harry. *A Childhood: The Biography of a Place.* New York: Harper and Row, 1978.

-------------- *Classic Crews.* New York: Touchstone, 1995.

Daly, Martin and Margo Wilson. "Risk of Maltreatment of Children Living with Stepparents." *Child Abuse and Neglect: Biosocial Dimensions.* Eds. R. Gelles and J. Lancaster. New York: Aldine de Gruyter, 1987.

Dickerson, James L. *Just for a Thrill: Lil Hardin Armstrong, First Lady of Jazz.* New York: Cooper Square Press, 2002.

--------------- *Faith Hill: Piece of My Heart.* New York: St. Martin's Press, 2001.
Douglas, Kirk. *The Ragman's Son.* New York: Pocket Books, 1988.

Duberman, Lucile. *The Reconstituted Family: A Study of Remarried Couples and Their Children.* Chicago, IL: Nelson-Hall, 1975.

Eliot, Lise. *What's Going on in there?: How the Brain and Mind Develop in the First Five Years of Life.* New York: Bantam, 1999.

Empfield, Maureen, and Nicholas Bakalar. *Understanding Teenage Depression.* New York: Henry Holt, 1999.

--------------- *Identity and the Life Cycle.* New York: W.W. Norton, reissued 1980.

Erickson, E.H. *Childhood and Society.* New York: W.W. Norton, 1963.

Farr, Finis. *John O'Hara: A Biography.* Boston: Little, Brown and Co., 1973.

Furstenberg, Frank F., and Andrew J. Cherlin. *Divided Families: What Happens to Children When Parents Part.* Cambridge, Mass.: Harvard University Press.

Garfinkel, Irwin and Sara S. McLanahan. *Single Mothers and Their Children.* Washington, DC: The Urban Institute Press, 1986.

Gelles, R. and J. Lancaster, eds. *Child Abuse and Neglect: Biosocial Dimensions.* New York: Aldine de Gruyter, 1987.

Glenn, John, with Nick Taylor. *John Glenn: A Memoir.* New York: Bantam Books, 1999.

Golding, William. *Lord of the Flies.* New York: Capicorn Books, 1959.

Hart, Henry. *James Dickey: The World as a Lie.* New York: Picador, 2000.

Hauser, Thomas. *Muhammad Ali: His Life and Times.* New York: Touchstone, 1991.

Hetherington, E. Mavis. *For Better O For Worse.* New York: W.W. Norton, 2002.

Ingersoll, Barbara D. and Sam Goldstein. *Lonely, Sad and Angry.* New York: Doubleday, 1995.

Kidman, Antony. *Family Life.* Sydney, Australia: Biochemical and General Services, 1995.

--------------- *From Thought to Action: A Self-Help Manual.* Sydney, Australia: Biochemical and General Services, 1988.

Kindlon, Dan, and Michael Thompson. *Raising Cain: Protecting the Emotional Life of Boys.* New York: Ballantine Books, 2000.

Klaus and J. Kennell. *Maternal-Infant Bonding.* St. Louis: Mosby, 1976.

Lamb, Michael. *The Role of the Father in Child Development.* New York: John Wiley, 1997.

Lamb, Michael and Ann Browns, eds. *Advances in Developmental Psychology.* Hillsdale, N.J.: Erlbaun.

Levine, Mel. *A Mind at a Time.* New York: Simon & Schuster, 2002.
Locke, John. Some Thoughts Concerning Education. New York: Oxford University Press, 1999.

McLanahan, Sara, and Gary Sandefur. *Growing Up with a Single Parent.* Cambridge, Mass.: Harvard University Press, 2001.

Macoby, Eleanor. *Social Development, Psychological Growth and Parent-Child Relations.* New York: Harcourt Brace Jovanovich, 1980.

Macoby, Eleanor Emmons and Carol Nagy Jacklin. *The Psychology of Sex Differences.* Stanford, California: Stanford University Press, 1974.

Maddi, Salvatore R. *Personality Theories: A Comparative Analysis.* Homewood, Illinois: Dorsey Press, 1976.

Michener, James A. *Sports in America.* New York: Random House, 1976.

Moustakas, Clark E. *Loneliness. "* Englewood Cliffs, NJ: Prentice-Hall, 1961.

Murphy, James M. *Coping With Teen Suicide.* New York: Rosen Publishing Group, 1999.

Neal, J.H. "Children's Understand of Their Parents' Divorces." In L. Kurdek, ed., *Children and Divorce: New Directions for Child Development.* San Francisco: Jossey-Bass, 1983.

Ogg, Alex, and David Upshal. *The Hip Hop Years.* New York: Fromm, 1999.
Osofsky, Joy. *Handbook of Infant Development.* New York: John Wiley & Sons, 1987.

Parini, Jay. *Robert Frost: A Life.* New York: Henry Holt and Co., 1999.

Piaget, Jean. *Six Psychological Studies.* New York: Random House, 1967.

--------------- *The Moral Judgment of the Child.* New York: Macmillan, 1932.

Popenoe, David. *Life Without Father.* New York: Martin Kessler Books / Free Press, 1996.

Prokop, Michael S. *Kids' Divorce Workbook.* Warren, Ohio: Alegra House, 1986.

Pruett, Kyle D. *The Nurturing Father: Journey Toward the Complete Man.* New York: Warner Books, 1988.

Riesman, David, with Nathan Glazer and Reuel Denny. *The Lonely Crowd: A Study of the Changing American Character.*_New Haven, Conn.: Yale University Press, 1950.

Rotundo, E. Anthony. American Manhood._New York: Basic Books, 1993.

Rousseau, Jean-Jacques. *Emile.* London: Oxford University Press, 1999.

Sartre, Jean-Paul. *The Words: The Autobiography.*_New York: Vintage Books, 1981.

Spence, Gerry. *A Boy's Summer: Fathers and Sons Together*. New York: St. Martin's Press, 2000.

Tanner. J. *Education and Physical Growth.*_London: Hodder and Stoughton, 1978.

Teyber, Edward. *Helping Children Cope with Divorce.*_San Francisco: Jossey-Bass, 1992.

Thomas, M. *Comparing Theories of Child Development.*_New York: W.W. Norton, 1996.

Thompson, Clara, Milton Mazer, and Earl Witenberg. *An Outline of Psychoanalysis.* New York: Modern Library, 1955.

Thompson, Michael. *Speaking of Boys.*_New York: Ballantine Books, 2000.

Trimble, Betty. *Tim McGraw: A Mother's Story.* Nashville: Eggman Publishing, 1996.

Wachtel, Ellen F. *Treating Troubled Children and Their Families.*_New York: Guilford Press, 1994.

Wallerstein, Judith, and Sandra Blakeslee. *Second Chances: Men, Women, and Children a Decade After Divorce.*_Boston: Houghton Mifflin, 1996.

Wallerstein, Judith, Julie M. Lewis and Sandra Blakeslee. *The Unexpected Legacy of Divorce.* New York: Hyperion, 2000.

Watnik, Webster. *Child Custody Made Simple.* Claremont, Calif.: Single Parent Press, 1997.

Wodrich, David L. *Children's Psychological Testing: A Guide for Nonpsychologists.* Baltimore: Paul H. Brookes Publishing, 1984.

JOURNALS, MAGAZINES AND NEWSPAPERS

Adams, Tim. "Elmore Leonard." The Observer." January 26, 2003.

Aitchison, Diana. "There's Good Cruise and Bad Cruise." *The Commercial Appeal,* December 5, 1992.

Alessandri, Steven M., and Robert H. Wozniak. "The Child's Awareness of Parental Beliefs concerning the Child: A Developmental Study." *Child Development,* 1987, volume 58.

Amato, Paul R. "Parental Divorce and Attitudes toward Marriage and Family Life." *Journal of Marriage and the Family*, May 1988.

Amato, Paul R., and Alan Booth. "The Legacy of Parents' Marital Discord: Consequences for Children's Marital Quality." *Journal of Personality and Social Psychology,* October 2001, Vol. 81, No. 4.

Beardslee, William R., and Stuart Goldman. "Living Beyond Sadness." *Newsweek,* September 22, 2003.

Belsky, Jay. "Parent, Infant, and Social-Contextual Antecendents of Father-Son Attachment Security." *Developmental Psychology,* September 1, 1996, Vol. 32, Issue 5.

Biskind, Peter. "The Return of Quentin Tarantino." *Vanity Fair,* October 2003.
Collis, Clark. "Tim McGraw." *Blender,* March 2003.

Connelly, Christopher. "Tom Cruise." *Rolling Stone,* 1986.

Cooper, Peter. "McGraw may face prison in assault case." *Nashville Tennessean,* June 6, 2000.

Cowley, Geoffrey. "Girls, Boys and Autism." *Newsweek,* September 8, 2003.

Draper, Patricia and Henry Harpending. *Journal of Anthropological Research,* 1982, volume 36, issue 3.

DiClemente, Ralph. "Study Finds Link Between Tap Videos and Violence." *American Journal of Public Health,* March 2003.

Harris, Judith Rich. "The Outcome of Parenting: What Do We Really Know?" *Journal of Personality,* June 2000.

Heyman, J. D. and Marianne V. Stochmal and Rebecca Paley. "Did bullying—or a mother's neglect—drive a 12-year-old boy to suicide?" *People,* October 20, 2003.

Hofferth, Sandra L. and Kermyt G. Anderson. "Are All Dads Equal? Biology Versus Marriage as a Basis for Paternal Investment. *Journal of Marriage and Family*, February 2003.

Horsburgh, Susan and Joanne Fowler. "Cause of Death: Suicide." *People* magazine, September 15, 2003.

Jameson, Marnell. "Little Women." *Los Angeles Times*, November 1, 1999.

Jaffee, S.R., T.E. Moffitt, A. Caspi, and A. Taylor. "Life With (or Without) Father: The Benefits of Living with Two Biological Parents Depend on the Father's Antisocial Behavior." *Child Development,* February 1, 2003.

Kerig, Patricia K., Philip A. Cowan and Carolyn Pape Cowan. "Marital Quality and Gender Differences in Parent-Child Interaction." *Developmental Psychology,* November 1, 1993.

Kroska, Amy. "Investigating Gender Differences in the Meaning of Household Chores and Child Care." *Journal of Marriage and Family*, May 2003.

Lykken, David. "Factory of Crime." *Psychological Inquiry,* 1997, volume 8.
--------------- "The Causes and Costs of Crime and a Controversial Cure." *Journal of Personality,* 2000, volume 63.

McWhorter, John H. "Rap Only Ruins." *New York Post*, August 10, 2003.

MacKinnon-Lewis, Carol, David Rabiner, and Rebecca Starnes. "Predicting Boys' Social Acceptance and Aggression." *Developmental Psychology,* May 1999, Vol. 35. No. 3.

Martin, Nicole. "Fears Over Lure of Rap's Violence and Obscenity." The Daily Telegraph, August 21, 2000.

Martinez, Charles R. "Preventing Problems with Boys' Noncompliance: Effect of a Parent Training Intervention for Divorcing Mothers." *Journal of Consulting and Clinical Psychology,* June 1, 2001, Vol. 69, Issue 3.

Montague, Diane P. F., and Arlene S. Walker-Andrews. "Mothers, Fathers, and Infants: The Role of Person Familiarity and Parental Involvement in Infants' Perception of Emotion Expressions." *Child Development,* September/October 2002.

National Institute of Child Development (NICHD). "Do Children's Attention Processes Mediate the Link Between Family Predictors and School Readiness?" *Developmental Psychology,* May 1, 2003.

Phares, Vicky. "Where's Poppa? A Relative Lack of Attention to the Role of Fathers in Child and Adolescent Psychopathology." *American Psychologist,* 1992.

Pettit, Gregory S., and Kenneth A. Dodge. "Violent Children: Bridging Development, Intervention, and Public Policy." *Developmental Psychology,* March 1, 2003.

Raab, Scott. "Mister Nice Guy." *Entertainment Weekly,* March 14, 2003.
Ross, Emma. "Study Says Broken Homes Harm Kids More." Associated Press, London, Janaury 24, 2003.

Samuels, Allison. "Time to Tell it Like it Is" *Newsweek,* March 3, 2003.

Scoop Editors. "Faith & Healing." *People,* June 16, 2003.

Socol, Gary. "The Nicole Kidman Nobody Knows." *McCall's,* May 1998.

Sylvester, Tom. "Eminem: Father of the Year?" *Fatherhood Today,* Fall 2002.

Toppo, Greg. "The Face of the American Teacher." *USA Today,* July 2, 2003.

Walton, G.E., N. J. Bower and T.G. Bower. "Recognition of Familiar Faces by Newborns." *Infant Behavior and Development,* number 15.

Wootton, Adrian. "Quentin Tarantino Interview." *The Guardian,* date not available.